International Human Rights Law and Discrimination Protections

Comparative Discrimination Law

Volumes published in this Brill Research Perspectives title are listed at *brill.com/rpcd*

International Human Rights Law and Discrimination Protections

A Comparison of Regional and National Responses

By

Mpoki Mwakagali

BRILL

LEIDEN | BOSTON

This paperback book edition is simultaneously published as issue 1.2 (2017) of *Comparative Discrimination Law*, DOI 10.1163/24522031-12340002.

Library of Congress Control Number: 2018931280

Typeface for the Latin, Greek, and Cyrillic scripts: "Brill". See and download: brill.com/brill-typeface.

ISBN 978-90-04-34546-1 (paperback)
ISBN 978-90-04-34547-8 (e-book)

Published by Koninklijke Brill NV, Leiden, The Netherlands.
Koninklijke Brill NV incorporates the imprints Brill, Brill Hes & De Graaf, Brill Nijhoff, Brill Rodopi, Brill Sense and Hotei Publishing.

This book is printed on acid-free paper and produced in a sustainable manner.

Contents

Abbreviations

ACHPR	African Convention on Human and Peoples' Rights
ACtHPR	African Court on Human and Peoples' Rights
AU	African Union
CEACR	ILO Committee of Experts on the Application of Conventions and Recommendations
CEDAW	Convention on the Elimination of All Forms of Discrimination Against Women
CERD	Committee on Elimination of Racial Discrimination
CESCR	Committee on Economic, Social and Cultural Rights
CLS	Core Labour Standards
CoE	Council of Europe
CRC	Convention on the Rights of the Child
CRPD	Convention on the Rights of Persons with Disabilities
CtEDAW	Committee on the Elimination of Discrimination Against Women
ECHR	European Convention on Human Rights
ECSR	European Committee of Social Rights
ECtHR	European Court of Human Rights
ESC	European Social Charter
EU	European Union
HRC	Human Rights Committee
ICCPR	International Covenant on Civil and Political Rights
ICERD	International Convention on the Elimination of All Forms of Racial Discrimination
ICESCR	International Covenant on Economic, Social and Cultural Rights
ILO	International Labour Organisation
OAU	Organisation of African Union
UDHR	Universal Declaration on Human Rights
UN	United Nations Organisation
UNGA	United Nations General Assembly

International Human Rights Law and Discrimination Protections

A Comparison of Regional and National Responses

Mpoki Mwakagali

Abstract

Non-discrimination is a fundamental principle of international human rights law. This volume discusses the international legal framework on this principle and comparatively elaborates the definition of discrimination as well as the grounds of discrimination in the various general and specialised international human rights treaties, including the International Labour Organisation conventions. The element of special measures as an integral aspect of this principle is also raised. A comparative discussion on the incorporation of international standards on the principle of non-discrimination established in the international treaties in regional as well as national human rights frameworks is also set forth to provide practical illustrations of the application of these standards in more specific and localised perspectives. Selected regional frameworks discussed are the African, American and European human rights regional frameworks and the national frameworks are South Africa and Brazil.

Keywords

human rights – principle of non-discrimination – equality – Universal Declaration on Human Rights – grounds of discrimination – discrimination in employment – special measures – affirmative action – obligations

Introduction

Non-discrimination is a fundamental principle of international human rights law as demonstrated by the vast body of human rights instruments: treaties, declarations, recommendations and other documents that incorporate the rights to non-discrimination and equality. There is an equally vast amount of

 | DOI 10.1163/9789004345478_002

jurisprudence on the interpretation of these rights by the various monitoring bodies of these international instruments. In essence, the principle of non-discrimination not only embraces the notion that all individuals must have their human rights equally respected, but also unites all human rights by ensuring that they apply to all persons without unwarranted exceptions.[1] Thus, this principle does not absolutely prohibit all forms of discrimination, but requires legal justification by a state for any discrimination against individuals belonging to a certain protected group.[2] When examining the justifications for discrimination, it is crucial to look into both positive measures and special measures such as affirmative action as aspects of the principle of non-discrimination. The former are obligations where a state is required to do something to prevent, redress or end discrimination, and the latter refers to actions taken to redress a history of discrimination in a manner that is limited in time or breadth.[3]

Two dimensions of the principle of non-discrimination can be found; non-discrimination and equality. These two terms are often used interchangeably and in essence are two sides of the same coin; negative and positive statements of the same principle:[4] "[O]ne is treated equally when one is not discriminated against and one is discriminated against when one is not treated equally".[5] Equality thus captures the positive dimension and non-discrimination captures the negative dimension, where the former encompasses duties to ensure equality and absence of discrimination and the latter abstention from discrimination.[6] The two also relate to each other in that equality is the goal of non-discrimination, whereas non-discrimination frames the legal or policy action used to achieve equality.[7] Non-discrimination cannot be applied independently as it is a qualifying principle pertaining the ways by which other rights and principles are applied, and thus should be understood in an adverbial way.[8]

---

1 Curtis Doebbler, The Principle of Non-Discrimination in International Law (Washington D.C.: CD Publishing, 2007), 1.

2 *Id.*

3 *Id.* at 13.

4 Samantha Besson, "The Principles of Non—Discrimination in the Convention on the Rights of the Child" in Michael Freeman (ed.) Children's Rights: Progress and Perspectives (The Netherlands: Brill/Nijhoff, 2011), 88.

5 *Id.*

6 *Id.*

7 Jarlath Clifford, "Equality" in Stephanie Farrior, Equality and Non-Discrimination under International Law, Volume 2 (New York: Ashgate, 2015).

8 Joseph Raz, The Morality of Freedom (Oxford: Clarendon, 1986), 230.

This volume discusses non-discrimination protections in the international human rights instruments, including the ILO's core labour standards as part of the general international human rights framework. It maps non-discrimination protections in these international instruments and also touches upon their interpretation by the respective monitoring mechanisms. This work then explores the application of these standards regionally and by two national legal frameworks, Brazil and South Africa, to compare the different approaches taken by certain states when implementing the international principle in national jurisdictions.

Part 1: Non-Discrimination and International Human Rights Law Protections: International Avenues

The United Nations

Up until World War II, the concept and scope of human rights suffered from conceptual and structural deficiencies. Although there were occasional popular upheavals, already arguably with the Magna Carta (1215) in England, then in the 18th century, the French Declaration of the Rights of Man and Citizen (1789) and the American Bill of Rights (1791), these were considered the exclusive concerns of the countries concerned.[9] The founding of the League of Nations after WWI did not quite solve the issues of social unrest. The enormity of human suffering during WWII and the creation of the United Nations (UN) laid the foundations of universality for human rights norms. As for discrimination and inequality issues, slavery, particularly in the United States, the Holocaust and more recently, apartheid in South Africa demonstrate how discrimination and inequality can involve the most insidious and egregious human rights problems and engender gross human rights abuses.[10] As a result of these abuses, legal measures have been adopted in modern times at the international level by the international community, the regional levels as well as the national level prohibiting discrimination on various grounds.

Coming to the issue of non-discrimination as a human right, the idea that the UN should become the international protector of the rights of the

9 The Hon Mr. Justice P. Nnaemeka-Agu, "Discrimination and the African Charter on Human and Peoples' Rights" 19:4 *Commonwealth Law Bulletin* (1993), 1670.

10 Lord Lester of Herne Hill QC, "Non-Discrimination in International Human Rights Law" in *Developing Human Rights Jurisprudence Volume 6: Sixth Judicial Colloquium on the Domestic Application of International Human Rights Norms* (London: The Commonwealth Secretariat, 1995), 10.

individual grew out of the tragic experiences of the Second World War and the horrendous violations of human rights committed in the Holocaust.[11] The preamble, which speaks of two wars that "have brought untold sorrow to mankind", reflects the principle of non-discrimination.[12] Unlike its predecessor, the League Covenant, whose foundational instruments lacked any mention of racial equality, the UN Charter sets forth its purposes as, among others,

> To develop friendly relations among nations based on respect for the principle of equal rights and self-determination of peoples[13] ... To achieve international co-operation in solving international problems of an economic, social, cultural, or humanitarian character, and in promoting and encouraging respect for human rights and for fundamental freedoms for all without distinction as to race, sex, language, or religion.[14]

In determining the functions and powers of the General Assembly, the Charter invokes the initiating of studies and recommendations promoting international action and assisting in the realization of human rights and fundamental freedoms for all without distinction as to race, sex, language, or religion.[15] It provides for the promotion of universal respect for, and observance of, human rights and fundamental freedoms for all without distinction as to race, sex, language, or religion.[16] The Charter, in purporting the basic objectives of the trusteeship system, which is established by the UN for the administration and supervision of territories placed under the UN's trusteeship by agreement, includes respect for human rights and fundamental freedoms for all without distinctions as to race, sex, language or religion.[17] Although the Charter does not create specific obligations, nor does it define human rights and fundamental freedoms, one thing is clear: the Charter explicitly prohibits discrimination as reflected in the Preamble, and this is one of the Charter's main principles.

The non-discrimination principle lies at the very heart of international human rights law because the core notion of human dignity it reflects underlies the very concept of human rights, and non-discrimination is so essential

11 Li Weiwei, "Equality and Non-Discrimination under International Human Rights Law", Research Notes No. 3(2004), 5.
12 *See* Preamble, Charter of the United Nations.
13 Art. 1(2), Charter of the United Nations, 1945.
14 *Id.* at Art. 1(3).
15 *Id.* at Art. 13(1).
16 *Id.* at Art. 55(c).
17 *Id.* at Art. 76(c).

to realizing other human rights.[18] The non-discrimination principle reflects the fact that often, people are subjected to human rights violations because of prejudice against them due to some characteristic that identifies them, such as, race, colour, religion or sex, thus discrimination is an attack on the very notion of human rights—a denial that everyone is equal in dignity and worth.[19]

The Universal Declaration of Human Rights

The Universal Declaration of Human Rights (UDHR) begins by asserting the equality, in freedom, dignity and right, of all people as a birth right.[20] All human beings are to be entitled to the rights and freedoms in the Declaration without distinction of any kind, such as race, colour, sex, language, religion, political or other opinion, national or social origin, property, birth or other status, nor on the basis of the political, jurisdictional or international status of the country or territory to which a person belongs, whether it be independent, trust, non-self-governing or under any other limitation of sovereignty.[21] The prohibition of "distinction of any kind" arguably could mean that no differences at all are to be tolerated.[22] However, the interpretations of this clause by various monitoring bodies provide a clearer view as discussed below. The Declaration protects more grounds of discrimination than those provided for by the UN Charter (race, sex, language or religion) and thus expanding the grounds. Article 7 is on equality before the law where all people are entitled, without any discrimination, to equal protection of the law, equal protection against any discrimination in violation of the Declaration and against any incitement to such discrimination.[23]

The UDHR is a legally non-binding document that states can sign, but not ratify, meaning that it does not create legal and enforceable obligations on states. However, it has inspired the drafting of various legally binding international treaties encompassing the rights provided in the Declaration. Its cruciality, therefore, in as far as international human rights are concerned cannot be understated.

---

18 Stephanie Farrior, "Color" in the Non-Discrimination Provisions of the Universal Declaration of Human Rights and the Two Covenants" 14:4 *Washington University Global Studies Review* (2015), 754.

19 *Id.*

20 Art. 1, Universal Declaration on Human Rights, 1948.

21 *Id.* at Art. 2.

22 Office of the High Commissioner for Human Rights, *Human Rights in the Administration of Justice: A Manual on Huma Rights for Judges, Prosecutors and Lawyers* (New York: United Nations, 2003), 636.

23 *Id.* at Art. 7.

The International Covenant on Civil and Political Rights

Non-discrimination, together with equality before the law and equal protection of the law without any discrimination, constitutes a basic and general principle relating to the protection of human rights[24] The 1966 International Covenant on Civil and Political Rights (ICCPR), being one of the "twin Covenants", embodies this principle into more comprehensive, legally binding rights and obligations. However, the ICCPR does not contain any definition of discrimination. The Human Rights Committee[25] (HRC) fills this gap by defining discrimination as any distinction, exclusion, restriction or preference which is based on any ground such as race, colour, sex, language, religion, political or other opinion, national or social origin, property, birth or other status, and which has the purpose or effect of nullifying or impairing the recognition, enjoyment or exercise by all persons, on an equal footing, of all rights and freedoms.[26]

The ICCPR contains the right to non-discrimination in two key provisions. First, Article 2 of the Covenant reads:

> Each State Party to the present Covenant undertakes to respect and to ensure to all individuals within its territory and subject to its jurisdiction the rights recognized in the present Covenant, without distinction of any kind, such as race, colour, sex, language, religion, political or other opinion, national or social origin, property, birth or other status.[27]

And Article 26 of the Covenant reads:

> All persons are equal before the law and are entitled without any discrimination to the equal protection of the law. In this respect, the law

24 Human Rights Committee, General Comment No. 18, Non-Discrimination, 10th November 1989, para. 1.

25 The Human Rights Committee is the Covenant's monitoring body, consisting of independent experts. State parties to the Covenant are obliged to submit regular reports to the Committee on how the rights therein are being implemented and the Committee, after examining the reports, addresses its concerns and recommendations in the form of "concluding observations". The Committee also publishes its interpretations of the content of human rights provisions, known as "general comments", on thematic issues. The First Optional Protocol to the Covenant gives the Committee competence to examine individual complaints with regard to alleged violations of the Covenant by State parties to the Protocol. *See* United Nations Human Rights Office of the High Commissioner, "Human Rights Committee", available at ohchr.org.

26 Human Rights Committee, General Comment No. 18: Non-Discrimination, 10th November 1989, para. 1.

27 Art. 2, ICCPR, 1966.

> shall prohibit any discrimination and guarantee to all persons equal and effective protection against discrimination on any ground such as race, colour, sex, language, religion, political or other opinion, national or social origin, property, birth or other status.

Although on the surface, these provisions seem to be analogous and put forth the same right, they are different in consideration of the scope of their application. On one hand, Article 2 limits the scope of the rights to be protected against discrimination to those provided for in the Covenant.[28] On the other hand, Article 26 in itself provides an autonomous right against discrimination not limited to those rights provided for in the Covenant. It rather prohibits discrimination in law or in fact in any field regulated or protected by public authorities and is thus concerned more with obligations imposed on State parties in regard to their legislation and the application thereof.[29] This means that when legislation is adopted by a State party, it must comply with the requirement of Article 26 in that its content should not be discriminatory.[30] Put simply, the text of Article 26 makes clear that its application extends beyond the rights in the Covenant, that is, the civil and political sphere and extends to the proscription of any discrimination. This could include discrimination in the exercise of the rights or freedoms enumerated within the ICCPR or ICESCR, as well as discrimination in the exercise of rights or freedoms enumerated within another regional or international instrument.[31] In *Broeks v The Netherlands*,[32] the HRC confirmed this interpretation. This case concerned gender-related distinctions in legislation providing for unemployment benefits. The Committee held that there was a violation of Article 26, notwithstanding that the complaint related to rights guaranteed by ICESCR rather than the ICCPR.[33] Similarly, in *Müller and Engelhard v Namibia*,[34] the HRC provided that to impose much more onerous conditions for choosing the wife's surname as a family name than was the case for choosing the husband's surname entails a violation of Article 26 ICCPR.

---

28 Human Rights Committee, General Comment 18, U.N.Doc. HRI/GEN/Rev. 1at 26 (1994), para. 12.

29 *Id.*

30 *Id.*

31 *See* Jason Pobjoy, "Treating Like Alike: The Principle of Non-Discrimination as a Tool to Mandate the Equal Treatment of Refugees and Beneficiaries of Complementary Protection" *34 Melbourne University Law Review* (2010), 205.

32 UN Doc. CCPR/C/29/D/172/1984.

33 *Id.* at 34.

34 Communication No. 919/2000, CCPR/C/74/D/919/2000.

Another aspect of the ICCPR is the list of grounds of discrimination. The general "other status" clause indicates a non-exhaustive list of grounds of discrimination where other grounds can be incorporated. For example, the HRC has found discrimination on the ground of nationality as a ground on "other status" in *Gueye and others v France*,[35] where the pensions of Senegalese soldiers in the French army were found to be less than those of the French soldiers with the same records in the same army. The right to non-discrimination cuts across other aspects in the Covenant. One such example is gender equality where state parties have an obligation to ensure the equal rights of men and women to the enjoyment of all the rights set forth in the Convention,[36] equality before the courts and tribunals,[37] and equal participation in public life of every citizen without any distinction in Article 2 and without unreasonable restriction.

As to equality before courts and tribunals, the Article serves as a procedural means to safeguard the rule of law and aims at ensuring the proper administration of justice. It also extends to judicial bodies entrusted with judicial tasks by domestic law.[38] The aspect of equality before courts and tribunals is based on two components; equal access and equality of arms. The former refers to entitlement to access to administration of justice whereby no individual is to be deprived in procedural terms of this right to claim justice. Again, this is not limited to citizens of a State party but to all who may find themselves in the territory of subject to the jurisdiction of the state party.[39] To exemplify, the barring of persons from bringing suit against any other person by reason of any of the grounds provided for in Article 2 is a violation of the Covenant.[40] Again, where attempts to access a competent court are systematically frustrated *de jure* or *de facto* violates the Covenant.[41] Coming to the latter, it means that the same procedural rights are to be provided to all parties unless distinctions are based on law and can be justified on objective and reasonable grounds,

35 UN Doc. CCPR/C/35/D/196/1985.

36 Art. 3, ICCPR, 1966.

37 *Id.* at Art. 14(1).

38 *Perner v Austria*, Communication No. 1015/2001, para. 9.2.

39 Human Rights Committee, General Comment No. 32, CCPR/C/GC/32, 23rd August 2007, para. 9.

40 *Ato del Allevanal v Peru*, Communication No. 202/1986, para. 10.2.

41 *Olo Bahamonde v Equatorial Guinea*, Communication No. 468/1991, para. 9.4. *See also* General Comment No. 32, para. 9.

not entailing actual disadvantage or unfairness to the defendant.[42] For example, the right of both parties to appeal a certain decision. An exclusive right of the prosecutor to appeal but not the defendant could be seen as a violation of the Covenant.[43]

As to gender equality, Article 3 of the Covenant prohibits discriminatory acts on the ground of sex. An important aspect in this respect is the embedment of inequality in the enjoyment of rights by women in tradition, history and culture, including religious attitudes.[44] Here, State parties are to ensure that traditional, historical, religious or cultural attitudes are not used to justify violations of women's rights to equality before the law and to equal enjoyment of all Covenant rights.[45] These aspects of tradition have been the source of or justifying factors behind gender discrimination.[46]

What is interesting is that the Committee requires State members to provide information on how certain rights in the Covenant are being implemented. For example, equal enjoyment of human rights by women during a state of emergency (Art. 4) where states are to submit information on all measures taken during such situation to protect women from rape, abduction and other forms of gender-based violence, as women are particularly vulnerable in times of internal and international armed conflict.[47] Similar is the right to life (Art. 6) where states are to provide data on birth rates and pregnancy and childbirth-related deaths of women. In addition, State parties are to report on measures to protect women from practices that violate their right to life, such as female infanticide, the burning of widows and dowry killings, as well as honour killings.[48] Finally, the significance of the right to non-discrimination as a central principle of the Covenant is clear. This is demonstrated by the wording of its Article 4 stipulating that even in times of public emergencies that threaten the very life and existence of a nation, the state parties can only take measures derogating from their obligations under the Covenant provided that

42 General Comment No. 32, para. 13. *See also Dudko v Australia*, Communication No. 1347/2005, para. 7.4.

43 *Robinson v Jamaica*, Communication No. 223/1987. *See also* General Comment No. 32, para. 4.

44 Human Rights Committee, General Comment No. 28, CCPR/C/21/Rev.1/Add.10, 29th March 2000, para. 5.

45 *Id.*

46 Relevant to Art. 25 of the ICCPR is the fact that up until 2015, women were not allowed to vote nor run for public office in elections in Saudi Arabia.

47 *Id.* at para. 8.

48 *Id.* at para. 10.

such measures, among other things (not inconsistent with their obligations under international law), do not involve discrimination solely on the ground of race, colour, sex, language, religion or social origin.[49]

As one of the aspects of the principle of non-discrimination is that of affirmative action, it is important to note that the Covenant does not contain any explicit provision on this aspect. However, the HRC has provided for affirmative action by stating that:

> The ... principle of equality sometimes requires States parties to take affirmative action in order to diminish or eliminate conditions which cause or help to perpetuate discrimination prohibited by the Covenant. For example, in a State where the general conditions of a certain part of the population prevent or impair their enjoyment of human rights, the State should take specific action to correct those conditions. Such action may involve granting for a time to the part of the population concerned certain preferential treatment in specific matters as compared with the rest of the population. However, as long as such action is needed to correct discrimination in fact, it is a case of legitimate differentiation under the Covenant.[50]

Although the HRC makes the point that positive measures are required to implement the non-discrimination obligations of States under the Convention, the content of such measures and the situations in which positive measures are to be taken are unclear.[51]

International Covenant on Economic, Social and Cultural Rights

The 1966 International Covenant on Economic, Social and Cultural Rights (ICESCR), adopted at the same time as the ICCPR, is another key international instrument providing for the right to non-discrimination. To begin with, this Covenant's preamble echoes the spirit of "equal and inalienable rights of all" proclaimed in the UN Charter.[52] The Covenant, like its twin, does not provide a definition of discrimination. However, the Committee on Economic, Social and Cultural Rights (CESCR) has adopted a definition of discrimination

49 Art. 4, ICCPR, 1966.

50 Human Rights Committee, General Comment No. 18 (non-discrimination), UN doc. HRI/GEN/1/Rev.9, para. 10.

51 *See* Manfred Nowak, *U.N. Covenant on Civil and Political Rights: CCPR Commentary* (Virginia: Engel Publishers, 2005), 476–478.

52 *See* Preamble, ICESCR, 1966.

similar to that of the Human Rights Committee. Discrimination is defined as constituting any distinction, exclusion, restriction or preference or other differential treatment that is directly or indirectly based on the prohibited grounds of discrimination and which has the intention or effect of nullifying or impairing the recognition, enjoyment or exercise, on an equal footing, of Covenant rights.[53] Critical to the fundamentality of the principle of non-discrimination is the notion put forward by the CESCR that as discrimination undermines the fulfilment of economic, social and cultural rights, non-discrimination and equality are fundamental components of international human rights law and essential to the enjoyment of the rights in the Covenant.[54]

Key to non-discrimination in the Covenant is article 2, which states that:

1. Each State Party to the present Covenant undertakes to take steps, individually and through international assistance and co-operation, especially economic and technical, to the maximum of its available resources, with a view to achieving progressively the full realization of the rights recognized in the present Covenant by all appropriate means, including particularly the adoption of legislative measures.[55]
2. The States Parties to the present Covenant undertake to guarantee that the rights enunciated in the present Covenant will be exercised without discrimination of any kind as to race, colour, sex, language, religion, political or other opinion, national or social origin, property, birth or other status.[56]

To begin with, as is the case with the ICCPR, the list of grounds of discrimination is not exhaustive in the ICESCR. The phrase "other status" leaves the list of discrimination grounds open-ended, leaving room for those grounds not explicitly mentioned to be considered prohibited grounds. This is confirmed by the CESCR, which has stated that the inclusion of "other status" indicates that the list is not exhaustive and other grounds may be incorporated in this category.[57] Article 2(2) ICESCR is analogous to Article 2 ICCPR and the

---

53 Committee on Economic, Social and Cultural Rights, General Comment No. 20 (art. 2, para. 2 of the International Covenant on Economic, Social and Cultural Rights, UN Doc. E/C.12/GC/20, 2nd July 2009, para. 7.

54 *Id.* at paras. 1–2.

55 Art. 2(1), International Covenant on Economic, Social and Cultural Rights, 1966.

56 *Id.* at Art. 2(2).

57 CESCR, General Comment No. 20 (Non-Discrimination in Economic, Social and Cultural Rights (Art. 2, para. 2 of the ICESCR), UN Doc. E/C.12/GC/20, para. 15.

prohibited grounds for discrimination are identical. However, the wording of the article indicates that the non-discrimination protections are limited to the rights encompassed in the Covenant.

In interpreting the two paragraphs of Article 2 ICESCR, the CESCR puts forth various interesting aspects of the right to protection against discrimination. First is the immediate versus progressive aspect in respect to the right as per article 2(1). Here, the Committee argues that:

> [T]he term "progressive realization" is often used to describe the intent of this phrase. The concept of progressive realization constitutes a recognition of the fact that full realization of all economic, social and cultural rights will generally not be able to be achieved in a short period of time. In this sense the obligation differs significantly from that contained in article 2 of the International Covenant on Civil and Political Rights which embodies an immediate obligation to respect and ensure all of the relevant rights. Nevertheless, the fact that realization over time, or in other words progressively, is foreseen under the Covenant should not be misinterpreted as depriving the obligation of all meaningful content ... States are responsible for progressive realization of these rights and must move as expeditiously and effectively as possible towards that goal.[58]

However, when it comes to non-discrimination, the CESCR has found that while the Covenant provides for progressive realization and acknowledges the constraints due to the limits of available resources, it also imposes various obligations which are of immediate effect; one of which is the "undertaking to guarantee" that relevant rights "will be exercised without discrimination."[59] Furthermore, the Committee has reinstated this position with regards to non-discrimination by stating that non-discrimination is an immediate and cross-cutting obligation in the Covenant where article 2(2) requires State parties to guarantee non-discrimination in the exercise of each of the economic, social and cultural rights enshrined in the Covenant.[60] A similar example is that of the right to education. Article 13 ICESCR provides that:

58 CESCR, General Comment No. 3; The Nature of State Parties' Obligations, UN Doc. E/1991/23, 1st January 1991, para. 9.

59 *Id.* at para. 1.

60 CESCR, General Comment No. 20 (Non-Discrimination in Economic, Social and Cultural Rights (Art. 2, para. 2 of the ICESCR), UN Doc. E/C.12/GC/20, para. 7.

> The States Parties to the present Covenant recognize the right of everyone to education. They agree that education shall be directed to the full development of the human personality and the sense of its dignity, and shall strengthen the respect for human rights and fundamental freedoms. They further agree that education shall enable all persons to participate effectively in a free society, promote understanding, tolerance and friendship among all nations and all racial, ethnic or religious groups, and further the activities of the United Nations for the maintenance of peace.[61]

In this respect, the CESCR has not classified the right to education as an economic, social and cultural right, but also as a civil and political right since it is central to the full and effective realization of those rights as well.[62] It has also highlighted the importance of education in empowering women, safeguarding children from exploitative and hazardous labour and sexual exploitation, amongst others.[63]

Similar to the ICCPR, the ICESCR lays emphasis on prohibiting discrimination on the ground of sex by providing for the duty of member states to ensure the equal right of men and women to the enjoyment of all the rights set forth in the Covenant.[64] This right is also found in the previously discussed UN treaties.[65] The CESCR has highlighted the importance of non-discrimination as fundamental to the enjoyment of these rights.[66]

Similar again to the ICCPR, the ICESCR brings up the aspect of discrimination as a result of custom where discrimination is often caused by attitudes which are firmly rooted in the customs of certain societies.[67] This form of

---

61 *Id.* at Art. 13(1).

62 CESCR, General Observation No. 11.

63 CESCR, General Comment No. 13: The Right to Education (Art. 13), E/C.12/1999/10, 8th December 1999, para. 1. Other rights that require immediate implementation as provided by General Comment No. 3 include equal rights of men and women in their enjoyment of economic, social and cultural rights (art. 3), equal remuneration for equal value of work (art. 7), the right to form and join trade unions and to strike (art. 8), protection of children from economic and social exploitation (art. 10), providing free and compulsory education (art. 13(2a)).

64 *Id.* at Art. 3.

65 *See* Art. 1(3), UN Charter; Art. 2, UDHR; Art. 3, ICCPR.

66 CESCR, General Comment No. 16 (art. 3), E/C.12/2005/4, 11th August 2005, para. 3.

67 An example is customary rules or laws that prohibit or hinder women from owning immovable property, from inheriting property or from participating in economic activities such as employment, etc. *See* Amanda Ellis et al., *Gender and Economic Growth in Tanzania: Creating Opportunities for Women* (Washington D.C.: The World Bank, 2007)

discrimination is linked to the traditions and the dominant values of the society in question and is usually widely accepted by the victims as a part of their specific culture. This kind of practice is referred to as culturally ingrained discrimination.[68]

Another crucial aspect of non-discrimination in the ICESCR is that of formal discrimination and substantive discrimination, also known as *de jure* equality and *de facto* equality respectively. The former has more to do with legislation and policy as a means to deal with non-discrimination while the latter is concerned with practice and the effects of the laws, policies and practices. The CESCR provides that eliminating the former requires ensuring that a State's constitution, laws and policy documents do not discriminate on prohibited grounds: for example, laws should not deny equal social security benefits to women on the basis of their marital status. On the other hand, with regards to the latter, is the notion that merely addressing the formal discrimination will not ensure substantive equality … eliminating discrimination in practice requires paying sufficient attention to groups of individuals which suffer historical or persistent prejudice instead of merely comparing the formal treatment of individuals in similar situations.[69] Here, circumstances where differential treatment does not amount to discrimination are put forward, that is, where the justification for differentiation is reasonable and objective.

Lastly is the issue of affirmative action. Similar to the ICCPR, the ICESCR does not contain any provisions on affirmative action nor positive measures. However, the CESCR has filled this gap by stating that:

> In order to eliminate substantive discrimination, States parties may be, and in some cases are, under an obligation to adopt special measures to attenuate or suppress conditions that perpetuate discrimination. Such measures are legitimate to the extent that they represent reasonable, objective and proportional means to redress *de facto* discrimination and are discontinued when substantive equality has been sustainably achieved. Such positive measures may exceptionally, however, need to

---

49–50; and Rachel Sieder and John-Andrew McNeish, *Gender Justice and Legal Pluralities: Latin American and African Perspectives* (New York: Routledge, 2013).

68 Barbara Wilson, "The Principle of Non-Discrimination in the International Covenant on Economic, Social and Cultural Rights" in Walter Kälin et al. (eds.), International Law, Conflict and Development: The Emergence of a Holistic Approach in International Affairs (Brill Online Books and Journals, DOI: 10.1163/ej.9789004178588.i-650, 219.

69 CESCR, General Comment No. 20, para. 8.

be of a permanent nature, such as interpretation services for linguistic minorities and reasonable accommodation of persons with sensory impairments in accessing health care facilities.[70]

Specialised International Human Rights Treaties

Specialised international human rights treaties are those dealing with a specific theme. In contrast to the general treaties as discussed above, these specialized treaties are more focused and specialized regarding issues of concern, for example, racial discrimination or torture, as well as social groups identified as requiring protection, such as children, women, persons with disabilities, migrants etc. In as far as the principle of non-discrimination is concerned, these treaties are important because they deal with specific grounds of discrimination such as gender, race, disability etc.

Convention on the Elimination of All Forms of Discrimination against Women

The 1979 Convention on the Elimination of All Forms of Discrimination Against Women (CEDAW) is the only international human rights instrument that focuses solely and comprehensively on women's human rights. Though these rights are also found in other human rights instruments, such as those discussed above as well as regional instruments, the CEDAW is unique as it penetrates substantially the boundaries of the private realm in which women are located in virtually all societies. CEDAW outlines both general and specific remedies for the systematic inequities and oppressive societal biases that limit women's participation and equal operation within state systems, forcing an interrogation of traditional norms and standards and requires each state party to assume an active role in eliminating and/or mitigating the gender-based inequitable treatment of its citizens.[71]

CEDAW's Preamble, like the other human rights treaties, resonates that "all human beings are born free and equal in dignity and rights," articulating the entitlement of everyone to all the rights and freedoms in the Convention without distinction of any kind, including distinction based on sex. Again, despite reiterating the obligations of State parties to ensure the equal rights of men and women in the International Covenants on Human Rights (the ICCPR and ICESCR) and other UN instruments, CEDAW takes up the continued existence of extensive discrimination against women as an obstacle to the participation

70 Id. at para. 10.

71 Diana Zoelle, *Globalising Concern for Women's Human Rights: The Failure of the American Model* (New York: St. Martin's Press, 2000), 5.

of women, on equal terms with men, in the political, economic, social and cultural life of their countries. Finally, of importance is the desired change in the traditional role of men as well as role of women in society and in the family needed to achieve full equality between men and women.[72]

CEDAW defines discrimination against women as "any distinction, exclusion or restriction made on the basis of sex which has the effect or purpose of impairing or nullifying the recognition, enjoyment or exercise by women, irrespective of their marital status, on a basis of equality of men and women, of human rights and fundamental freedoms in the political, economic, social, cultural, civil or any other field."[73] The Convention places very clear obligations on the State parties, requiring the condemnation of discrimination against women in all its forms by taking measures to embody the principle of the equality of men and women in national constitutions and other appropriate legislation and to ensure, through such, practical realization of this principle. There is in addition an obligation for the State parties to adopt appropriate legislative measures; to establish legal protection of such rights through competent national tribunals and other public institutions.[74] This obligation ensures the existence of institutions to adjudicate any actions inconsistent with the rights in the Convention.[75] Another obligation is to refrain from engaging in any act or practice of discrimination against women and ensure that public authorities act in conformity with this obligation.[76]

When it comes to the obligation to take appropriate measures to eliminate discrimination against women by any person, organization or enterprise,[77] the Convention extends beyond the public realm and covers even those actions that are not of the State itself, but are by other agents both public and private, be it individuals, organisations or enterprise. In *Da Silva Pimentel Teixeira v Brazil*,[78] the applicant's daughter, being of African descent and from a lower socio-economic background, received inadequate care when she suffered a miscarriage, including surgery in an ill-equipped private clinic, and

---

72 *See* Preamble, Convention on the Elimination of All Forms of Discrimination Against Women, 1979.

73 *Id.* at Art. 1.

74 *Id.* at Art. 2(c).

75 See Committee on the Elimination of Discrimination Against Women, Implementation of Article 21 of the Convention on the Elimination of All Forms of Discrimination Against Women, Analysis of Article 2 of the Convention, Report of the Secretariat, 14th session, 16th January–3rd February 1995, at para. 40.

76 *Id.* at Art. 2(d).

77 *Id.* at Art. 2(e).

78 CEDAW/C/49/D/17/2008, 27th September 2011.

subsequently died. Domestic proceedings brought by the applicant had not been resolved eight years later at the time of the hearing by the Committee. The State agreed that the victim did not receive the individualized treatment she needed. The Committee concluded that the victim was indeed discriminated against. In addition, it concluded that the State had violated its obligations under, among others, article 2(c) by failing to provide access to justice for the victim[79] as well as article 2(e) in relation to its due diligence obligation to regulate the activities of private health service providers.[80] State parties are obliged to take appropriate measures to modify or abolish existing laws, regulations, customs and practices which constitute discrimination against women and to repeal penal provisions which constitute discrimination against women.[81]

The convention also places obligations on State parties to take appropriate measures to eliminate discrimination against women in political and public life[82] including the opportunity to represent their governments at the international level,[83] retainment of nationality,[84] education,[85] employment,[86] health care,[87] economic and social life,[88] marriage and family relations[89] as well as equality before the law.[90]

The Convention also places the obligation on State parties to take appropriate measures to achieve the elimination of prejudices and customary and all practices which are based on the idea of the inferiority or superiority of

79 *Id.* at para. 7.8, 8.

80 *Id.* at para. 7.5, 8.

81 *Id.* at Art. 2(f)–(g).

82 *Id.* Art. 7.

83 *Id.* at Art. 8.

84 *Id.* at Art. 9.

85 *Id.* at Art. 10. The provision on education is interesting as it covers not only formal education and vocational training, but also extends to educational information to ensure the health and well-being of families as well as information and advice on family planning. In *A.S v Hungary* (CEDAW/C/36/D/4/2004), the applicant was subjected to sterilization without informed consent at a Hungarian hospital during an emergency caesarean sec. procedure, mainly because she had given written consent to tubal ligation by signing a document that described the procedure in words she did not understand. The Committee found that the State party failed through the hospital personnel to provide appropriate information and advice on family planning, thus violated Art. 10(h) of the Convention.

86 *Id.* at Art. 11. The Committee has noted that the ratification of the ILO Convention No. 111 is crucial to the full implementation of this right as provided for by the CEDAW.

87 *Id.* at Art. 12.

88 *Id.* at Art. 13.

89 *Id.* at Art. 16.

90 *Id.* at Art. 15.

either of the sexes or on stereotyped roles for men and women as well as ensure, along with maternity as a social function, recognition of the common responsibility of men and women in the upbringing and development of their children.[91] Finally, the state parties are to take all appropriate measures, including legislation, to suppress all forms of traffic in women and exploitation of prostitution of women.[92]

Coming to the issue of affirmative action, the Convention also provides for differential treatment which does not amount to discrimination. Article 4 of the Convention states:

1. Adoption by States Parties of temporary special measures aimed at accelerating de facto equality between men and women shall not be considered discrimination as defined in the present Convention, but shall in no way entail as a consequence the maintenance of unequal or separate standards; these measures shall be discontinued when the objectives of equality of opportunity and treatment have been achieved.
2. Adoption by States Parties of special measures, including those measures contained in the present Convention, aimed at protecting maternity shall not be considered discriminatory.

The Committee on the Elimination of Discrimination Against Women (CtEDAW) has stated that in as far as substantive equality is concerned, it is not enough to guarantee women treatment that is identical to that of men. Rather, biological as well as socially and culturally constructed differences between women and men must be taken into account and the non-identical treatment of women and men will be required in order to address such differences.[93] The CtEDAW views the application of such measures not as an exception to the norm of non-discrimination, but rather as an emphasis that temporary special measures are part of a necessary strategy by States parties directed towards the achievement of de facto or substantive equality of women with men in the enjoyment of their human rights and fundamental freedoms.[94] Moreover, the Committee, while emphasizing the temporary nature of such measures, elaborates on these measures as to encompass a wide variety of

---

91 *Id.* at Art. 5.

92 *Id.* at Art. 6.

93 Committee on Elimination of Discrimination Against Women, General Recommendation No. 25: Art. 4, paragraph 1 of the Convention (temporary special measures), 30th Session, 2004, para. 8.

94 *Id.* at para. 18.

legislative, executive, administrative and other regulatory instruments, policies and practices, such as outreach or support programmes, allocation and/or reallocation of resources, preferential treatment, targeted recruitment, hiring and promotion, numerical goals connected with time frames, and quota systems. The choice of a particular "measure" will depend on the context in which article 4(1) CEDAW is applied and on the specific goal it aims to achieve.[95] An example of such special measures can be seen in the case of Japan, where special measures were taken to enhance the participation of women in decision-making processes by allotting gender quotas for recruitment of women in various national advisory councils and committees.[96]

Convention on the Elimination of All Forms of Racial Discrimination

As is with various human rights instruments, various events led to the adoption of the 1965 Convention on the Elimination of All Forms of Racial Discrimination (ICERD). One of these was an epidemic of swastika—painting and other "manifestations of anti—Semitism and other forms of racial and national hatred and religious and racial prejudices of similar nature."[97]

ICERD's preamble incorporates various international human rights instruments that protect the right to equality, including the UDHR, the Declaration on the Elimination of all Forms of Racial Discrimination as well as the ILO core labour Convention on Discrimination in Respect of Employment and Occupation (No. 111) and the Convention Against Discrimination in Education (UNESCO). ICERD emphasizes that all human beings are equal before the law and are entitled to equal protection of the law against any discrimination and against any incitement to discrimination.[98]

The convention defines racial discrimination to mean:

> [A]ny distinction, exclusion, restriction or preference based on race, colour, descent, or national or ethnic origin which has the purpose or effect of nullifying or impairing the recognition, enjoyment or exercise, on an equal footing, of human rights and fundamental freedoms in the political, economic, social, cultural or any other field of public life.[99]

95 *Id.* at para. 22.

96 *See* Japan's Fifth Periodic Report, CEDAW/C/JPN/5, 13th September 2002.

97 Egon Schwelb, "The International Convention on the Elimination of All Forms of Racial Discrimination" 15:4 *International and Comparative Law Quarterly* (1966), 997.

98 Preamble, ICERD.

99 Art. 1(1), ICERD.

However, some exceptions to the definition include distinctions, exclusions, restriction or preferences between citizens and non-citizens made by a state party as well as special measures taken for the advancement of certain racial or ethnic groups requiring such protection.[100]

Article 1 of the ICERD puts forth the conditions for which acts (distinctions, exclusion, restrictions or preferences) can be considered discriminatory in the sense of the convention. First, such acts should be based on race, colour, descent national origin or ethnic origin and second, the acts should have the *purpose* of nullifying or impairing the recognition, enjoyment or exercise or exercise, on an equal footing, of human rights and fundamental freedoms in the political, economic, social, cultural or any other field of public life, or have such an *effect*.[101] ICERD does not prohibit distinctions based on whether a person is a citizen of a country or not, but rather distinctions based on race, colour descent or national or ethnic origin also in regards to foreigners.[102]

ICERD places obligations on member states to not only condemn racial discrimination but to also take up appropriate and prompt policy of eliminating racial discrimination, including public authorities and institutions. Again is the obligation not to sponsor, defend or support racial discrimination by any person or organization as well as prohibit or bring to an end racial discrimination by any person, group or organization. It also obliges states to take effective measures to ensure protection of certain racial group or individuals, belonging to them for the purpose of guaranteeing them the full and equal enjoyment of human rights and fundamental freedom.[103] The convention also condemns racial segregation and apartheid and undertakes to prevent, prohibit and eradicate all practices of this nature.

Article 4 ICERD obliges states to condemn all propaganda and all organisations based on ideas or theories of superiority of one race of group of persons of one colour, ethnicity or origin or which attempts to justify or promote racial hatred and discrimination in any forms by dissemination of ideas based on racial superiority or incitement to racial discrimination and the provision of any assistance to racist activities, punishable by law. ICERD also requires states to declare illegal and prohibit organizations which promote and incite racial

---

100 Article 1(2–4).

101 See Natan Lerner, *The UN Convention on the Elimination of all forms of Racial Discrimination* (Boston: Nijohoff, 2015), 35.

102 Egon Schwelb, 1007.

103 Art. 2(2) ICERD.

discrimination as well as make participation in is such organisations punishable by law.[104]

The convention also obliges states to prohibit and eliminate racial discrimination in all forms and guarantee the rights to equality before the law without distinction as to race, colour or national or ethnic origin.[105] The convention provides for access to justice, access to remedies through competent national tribunals and other institutions against any acts of discrimination which violate their human rights and fundamental freedoms.[106]

Article 7 provides for the adoption of measures in the field of teaching, education and culture and for information with a view of combating those prejudices that lead to racial discrimination and to promoting understanding tolerance and friendship among nations and racial and ethnical groups and propagating the purpose and principles of character of the United Nations, the UDHR, the Declaration on ERD and the Convention.[107]

Affirmative action is addressed in Article 1(4) ICERD, which requires that special measures be taken for the sole purpose of securing adequate advancement of certain racial or ethnic groups or individuals requiring such protection as may be necessary in order to ensure such groups or individuals equal enjoyment or exercise of human rights and fundamental freedoms. Such measures are not to lead to the maintenance of separate rights for different racial groups and that they are not to be continued after the objectives for which they were taken have been achieved. The Committee on Elimination of Racial Discrimination has clarified the notion of "adequate advancement" to mean goal-directed programmes that:

> [H]ave the objective of alleviating and remedying disparities in the enjoyment of human rights and fundamental freedoms affecting particular groups and individuals ... include but are not confined to persistent or structural disparities and de facto inequalities resulting from the circumstances of history that continue to deny to vulnerable groups and individuals the advantages essential for the full development of the human personality.[108]

---

104 Art. 4.

105 Art. 5.

106 Art. 6.

107 Art. 7 ICERD.

108 Committee on the Elimination of Racial Discrimination, General Recommendation No. 32: The Meaning and Scope of Special Measures in the International Convention on

The Committee also states that it is not necessary to prove such "historic" discrimination in order to validate a programme of special measures, but rather emphasis is to be placed on correcting present disparities and on preventing further imbalances from arising.[109] It is crucial to bear in mind that ICERD only deals with racial discrimination. Therefore, the other grounds of discrimination found in various Human Rights instruments such as sex, religion, social origin, political opinion etc. are outside its scope.

Since its adoption in 1965, ICERD has had an impact at both national and international levels. ICERD pushed states to incorporate the rights into the constitutions in the national/domestic law. As examples, Sweden, which was one of the countries to declare recognition of the competence of the Committee under Article 14 of the convention, appointed a governmental commission to review existing legislations to ascertain the extent to which it met the requirement of the convention. Amendment has been made to the penal code to bring it in line with the Convention.[110] Similar examples can be found in New Zealand,[111] Greece[112] and France.[113]

At the international level, ICERD has promoted the adoption of several other instruments. For example, the preamble to the 1978 UNESCO Declaration on Race and Racial Prejudice states that it promotes the implementation of ICERD. The preamble to the International Convention on the Suppression and Punishment of the Crime of Apartheid, adopted in 1973, refers to and cites Article 3 ICERD. The Committee on the Elimination of Racial Discrimination (CERD) is the body monitoring states compliance with the convention.

Convention on the Rights of the Child

The existence of the 1989 Convention on the Rights of the Child (CRC) is not premised on an assumption that children are not protected from discrimination by all the human rights instruments discussed above. What is key with the CRC is the issue of vulnerability of children vis-a-vis the state, their families and other individuals, for example, Article 24(1) ICCPR and Article 10(3) ICESCR provide for discrimination in specific cases of children. The perception, however, was that protection of children against child-specific discrimination

---

Elimination of Racial Discrimination, 75th session, August 2009, UN doc. CERD/C/GC/32, paras. 21–22.

109 *Id.*

110 Nathan Learner at 195. *See also* CERD/C/R.50/Add.2 (Report submitted by Sweden).

111 CERD/C/R.50/Add. 8.

112 CERD/C/R.25/Add. 1 and Add. 7.

113 CERD/C/R.33/Add. 6.

called for the need of a specialized international instrument. The CRC complements and anchors obligations with regards to children as already enshrined in the Declaration on the Rights of the Child, but now in a legally-binding international human rights instrument.[114] The Convention is supplemented by three additional protocols relating to children in armed conflicts, sale of children, child prostitution and child pornography and lastly on communication procedures. The significance of the Convention is marked by its universal acceptance as shown by its wide ratification/accession, with approximately 196 state parties,[115] making it the most-widely ratified international human rights treaty in the world.

The CRC defines a "child" as any human being below the age of 18 years, except when national law determines an earlier age.[116] Central to non-discrimination in the convention is Article 2 which states:

1. States Parties shall respect and ensure the rights set forth in the present Convention to each child within their jurisdiction without discrimination of any kind, irrespective of the child's or his or her parent's or legal guardian's race, colour, sex, language, religion, political or other opinion, national, ethnic or social origin, property, disability, birth or other status.
2. States Parties shall take all appropriate measures to ensure that the child is protected against all forms of discrimination or punishment on the basis of the status, activities, expressed opinions, or beliefs of the child's parents, legal guardians, or family members.

This clause is vital in that it not only includes the grounds of discrimination found in all the other human rights instruments save for the addition of disability, but also addresses the "child's or his or her parent's or legal guardians race, colour ...", highlighting the dependency of children and also the problems of associational discrimination. Again, while the first paragraph covers the rights in the convention, the second one refers to any kind of discrimination and is autonomous, similar to articles 2(1) and 26 ICCPR respectively.

---

114 Eugeen Verhellen, "The Convention on the Rights of the Child: Reflections from a Historical, Social Policy and Educational Perspective" in Wouter Vandenhole et al. (eds.) *Routledge International Handbook of Children's Rights Studies* (New York: Routledge, 2015), 43.

115 See United Nations Treaty Collection available at treaties.un.org.

116 Art. 1, Convention on the Rights of the Child, 1989.

The obligations of state Parties are provided for in article 4 CRC, which reads:

> States Parties shall undertake all appropriate legislative, administrative, and other measures for the implementation of the rights recognized in the present Convention. With regard to economic, social and cultural rights, States Parties shall undertake such measures to the maximum extent of their available resources and, where needed, within the framework of international co-operation.

The Committee on the Rights of the Child has interpreted this article to elaborate such legislative and administrative measures. In the case of the former, it includes comprehensive and continuous review of all domestic legislation to ensure full compliance with the Convention.[117] As to the latter, these comprise cross-sectoral coordinations across government and between different levels of government and between government and civil society, including in particular children themselves, as well as rigorous implementation by not only government institutions, but also independent human rights institutions and non-governmental organisations (NGOs).[118]

The second part of Article 4 CRC calls forth the civil and political versus economic, social and cultural rights divide when it refers to "the maximum extent of their available resources". The Committee has stated that this clause reflects a realistic acceptance that lack of resources—financial and otherwise—can hamper the full implementation of economic, social and cultural rights in some States, thus the introduction of the concept of "progressive realization" of such rights. In this scenario, the Committee has concurred with the Committee on Economic, Social and Cultural Rights in that "even where available sources are demonstrably inadequate, the obligation remains for a State party to strive to ensure the widest possible enjoyment of the relevant rights under the prevailing circumstances."[119] Here, although the CRC is very comprehensive and covers civil, political, economic, social and cultural rights, the relatively weaker protection of economic, social and cultural rights is apparent. However, the Committee on the Rights of the Child has clarified that as to

117 Committee on the Rights of the Child, General Comment No. 5—General Measures of Implementation of the Convention on the Rights of the Child (October 2003), Doc. CRC/GC/2003/5, para. 18.

118 *Id.* at para. 27.

119 *Id.* at para. 8.

progressive realization, states cannot indefinitely postpone realization because they are under obligation to take immediate steps towards full realization.[120]

The CRC rights themselves can be grouped into three categories; provision[121] (the right to get basic needs), protection (the right to be shielded from harmful acts) and participation (the right to be heard on discussions affecting the child's life).[122] The first category of rights on provision comprises rights such as the right to life, survival and development (art. 6) the right to health (art. 24), the right to education (art. 28) and the right to an adequate standard of living (art. 27). The second category of rights on protection includes, for example, protection against economic exploitation (art. 32), illicit use of drugs and narcotics (art. 33), physical and mental abuse (art. 19), illicit transfer (art. 11), interference with privacy (art. 16), sexual exploitation (art. 34), traffic of children (art. 35), torture, inhuman and degrading treatment (art. 37), and the use of children in armed conflict (art. 38). The third category of rights on participation includes the right to be heard (art. 12), freedom of expression (art. 13) and the right of access to information (art. 17). The Committee on the Rights of the Child has identified the general principles of the Convention to be articles 2 (non-discrimination), 3 (best interest of the child) and 12 (respect of the views of the child).[123]

The CRC, unlike the other specialized conventions but like the ICCPR and ICESCR, does not contain an explicit clause on affirmative action. However, various clauses as well as concluding observations can assist in deducing this aspect in as far as the Convention is concerned. First of all, the Preamble of the CRC recognizes that "in all countries in the world, there are children living in exceptionally difficult conditions, and that such children need special consideration",[124] clearly showing a stance towards special treatment or consideration of these children. Second, in terms of international law, the obligation to "respect" arguably requires states to refrain from any actions that would violate any of the rights of the child under the Convention. The obligation to "ensure" goes well beyond that of to "respect" since it implies an affirmative obligation on the part of the State to take whatever measures necessary to enable

120 Committee on Economic, Social and Cultural Rights, General Comment No. 3—The Nature of States Parties Obligations (Art. 2, para. 1), 1990.

121 This category of rights is also referred to as survival and development rights. See "Rights under the Convention on the Rights of the Child" available at unicef.org.

122 Thomas Hammarberg, "The UN Convention on the Rights of the Child—and How to Make It Work", 12 *Human Rights Quarterly* (1990), 100.

123 *Report of the Committee on the Rights of the Child*, UN Doc. A/55/41, 2000, para. 26.

124 Preamble, Convention on the Rights of the Child, 1989.

individuals to enjoy the relevant rights.[125] Finally, the concluding observations of the Committee on the Rights of the Child in country periodic reports provide for the obligations of member states to take affirmative measures. In its concluding observations in Sweden's report, the Committee required the government to "place particular focus on preventive activities against discrimination and, if necessary, take affirmative action for the benefit of children in vulnerable situations, including children from marginalised and disadvantaged families, a migration background, Roma …"[126]

Convention on the Rights of Persons with Disabilities

The 2006 Convention on the Rights of Persons with Disabilities (CRPD) is the first international human rights treaty to specifically, expressly and comprehensively protect the rights of persons with disabilities. Prior to its adoption, the Declaration on the Rights of Disabled People[127] was the first international document to incorporate the rights of persons with disabilities in general.[128] This document embraced the principle of non-discrimination from international human rights instruments such as the UDHR, ICCPR, ICESCR and the ILO international labour standards (the ILO constitution, conventions, recommendations and resolutions). However, in addition to its status as a non-binding document, the Declaration falls short of affirming unequivocally the right of all people with disabilities to substantive equality as a matter of international human rights law.[129]

---

125 Philip Alston, "The Legal Framework of the Convention on the Right of the Child", 91:2 *United Nations Bulletin of Human Rights* (1992), 5.

126 Committee on the Rights of the Child, Concluding Observation on the Fifth Periodic Report of Sweden, 68th session, UN doc. CRC/C/SWE/CO/4, para. 16(b). *See also* the Committee's concluding observations on Ghana's report, where it was concluded that "The Committee recommends that the State Party pay particular attention to the implementation of art. 4 of the Convention by increasing and prioritizing budgetary allocations to ensure at all levels the implementation of the rights of the child and that particular attention is paid to the protection of the rights of children belonging to vulnerable groups including children with disabilities, children affected or/and infected by HIV/AIDS, street children and children living in poverty …" at CRC/C/GHA/CO/2.

127 General Assembly Resolution 3447 (XXX) of 9th December 1975.

128 The Declaration on the Rights of Mentally Retarded Persons, 1971 was specifically on this category of persons and did not cover all persons with disabilities.

129 *See* Arlene S. Kanter, "A Comparative View of Equality under the UN Convention on the Rights of Persons with Disabilities and the Disabilities Laws of the United States and Canada" 32 *Windsor Year Book of Access to Justice* (2015), 70.

Coming to the CRPD, the preamble begins by recalling the principle of equality as proclaimed in the UN Charter as to the equality of all members as the human family, as well as recognizing the entitlement of everyone to all the rights and freedoms in the UDHR, ICCPR and ICESCR. In addition is the need for persons with disabilities to be guaranteed their full enjoyment without discrimination. The preamble also refers to various international human rights treaties and highlights the subjection of persons with disabilities to multiple or aggravated forms of discrimination.[130] However, it is imperative to highlight that, despite this reference to the general as well as specialized international human rights instruments, in as far as international human rights treaties are concerned, disability has not been given due regard. None of the non-discrimination clauses in the treaties discussed herein specifically mention disability in the grounds of discrimination, save for the CRC, although the "or other status" clause is interpreted to extend the protections of the rights in these treaties to persons with disabilities. However, this underscores the manner by which persons with disabilities have been tucked away in saving clauses and side-lined in resolutions and declarations, contributing significantly to the invisibility of persons with disabilities in the human rights discourse.[131]

Central to concepts of disability is the notion of systemic disadvantage, according to which persons with disability are discriminated against by social structures that segregate or exclude them from participating fully in society. This results in oppression by social structures and practices, both on the individual by diminishing or denying personhood and systematically by denying or diminishing civic participation on those labelled 'disabled'.[132] The underlying factor to this notion is traditional perceptions of disability, which have been oriented towards a medical or diagnostic model which focuses on the physical or intellectual limitation of persons with disabilities and consequently rely on medical intervention or the provision of technical aids as the major means of improving the lives of persons with disabilities.[133] The UN has underlined the importance of the Convention in moving away from these perceptions in that,

---

130 Preamble, Convention on the Rights of Persons with Disabilities, 2005.

131 *See* Marianne Schulze, *Understanding the United Nations Convention on the Rights of Persons with Disabilities* (Lyon: Handicap International, 2009), 10.

132 Rosemary Kayers and Phillip French, "Out of Darkness into the Light? Introducing the Convention on the Rights of Persons with Disabilities" *Human Rights Law Review* (2008), 5.

133 Jarna Petman, "The Special Reaching for the Universal: Why a Special Convention for Persons with Disabilities" in Jukka Kumpuvuori and Martin Scheinin (eds.) *United Nations Convention on the Rights of Persons with Disabilities-Multidisciplinary Perspectives* (Finland: Center for the Human Rights of Persons with Disabilities in Finland, 2009), 25.

> The Convention is a paradigm shift in approaches to disability, moving from a model where persons with disabilities are treated as objects of medical treatment, charity and social protection to a model where persons with disabilities are recognized as subjects of human rights, active in the decisions that affect their lives and empowered to claim their rights. This approach views the societal barriers—such as physical obstacles and negative attitudes—confronting persons with disabilities as the main obstacles to the full enjoyment of human rights.[134]

The purpose of the CRPD, therefore, is to promote, protect and ensure the full and equal enjoyment of all human rights and fundamental freedoms by all persons with disabilities. This includes persons with long-term physical, mental, intellectual or sensory impairments that in interaction with various barriers may hinder their full and effective participation in society on an equal basis with others and to promote respect for their inherent dignity.[135] Coming to the non-discrimination rights of persons with disabilities, discrimination on the basis of disability is defined in its Article 2(1) as "any distinction, exclusion or restriction on the basis of disability which has the purpose or effect of impairing or nullifying the recognition, enjoyment or exercise, on an equal basis with others, of all human rights and fundamental freedoms in the political, economic, social, cultural, civil or any other field. It includes all forms of discrimination, including denial of reasonable accommodation." Reasonable accommodation is the any necessary and appropriate modification and adjustments not imposing a disproportionate or undue burden, where needed in a particular case, to ensure to persons with disabilities the enjoyment or exercise on an equal basis with others of all human rights and fundamental freedoms.[136]

The CRPD places obligations on State parties to adopt all appropriate legislative, administrative and other measures for the implementation of the rights recognized in the Convention. The State parties are to take appropriate measures, including legislation, to modify or abolish existing laws, regulations, customs and practices that constitute discrimination against persons with disabilities; to take into account the protection and promotion of the human rights of persons with disabilities in all policies and programmes; to refrain from engaging in any act or practice that is inconsistent with the present Convention and to ensure that public authorities and institutions act in

134 United Nations, *Convention on the Rights of Persons with Disabilities: Advocacy Toolkit, Professional Training Series No. 15* (New York: United Nations, 2008), 7.

135 Art. 1, CRPD.

136 *Id.* at Art. 2(1).

conformity with the present Convention. State parties are also to take all appropriate measures to eliminate discrimination on the basis of disability by any person, organization or private enterprise; to undertake or promote research and development of universally designed goods, services, equipment and facilities and new technologies and to provide accessible information to persons with disabilities about mobility aids and other forms of assistance, support services and facilities.

The Convention, similar to the ICESCR and CRC, provides for the progressive realization of the economic, social and cultural rights in the CRPD, where State parties are to "take measures to the maximum of available resources ... with a view to achieving progressively the full realization of the rights, without prejudice to those obligations that are immediately applicable to international law."[137]

When it comes to the CRPD's substantive rights, these are identical to those found in the Bill of Rights and the specialized conventions and include the right to life (art. 10), equal recognition before the law (art. 12), access to justice (art. 13), freedom from torture or cruel, inhuman or degrading treatment or punishment (art. 15), freedom from exploitation (art. 16), freedom of expression (art. 21), right to privacy (art. 22), the right to education (art. 24), the right to health (art. 25), the right to work and employment (art. 27), adequate standard of living (art. 28), participation in political life (art. 29), participation in cultural life, recreation, leisure and sport (art. 30), etc. The Convention does not create new rights for this category of persons, but rather creates specific obligations on state parties to ensure that necessary measures are taken so that persons with disabilities can equally enjoy these international human rights.

Affirmative action is taken up in Article 5(4) which states that specific measures which are necessary to accelerate or achieve de facto equality of persons with disabilities shall not be considered discrimination under the terms of the present Convention. Affirmative action specific to work and employment is found in Article 27, which states:

1. States Parties recognize the right of persons with disabilities to work, on an equal basis with others; this includes the right to the opportunity to gain a living by work freely chosen or accepted in a labour market and work environment that is open, inclusive and accessible to persons with disabilities. States Parties shall safeguard and promote the realization of the right to work, including for those who acquire a disability during the

137 *Id.* at Art. 2(2).

course of employment, by taking appropriate steps, including through legislation, to, inter alia:

(h) Promote the employment of persons with disabilities in the private sector through appropriate policies and measures, which may include affirmative action programmes, incentives and other measures

This article does not just a prohibit discrimination on the ground of disability in the workplace, but also recognizes the right of persons with disabilities to work on an equal basis with others in the labour market. This is particularly important as discrimination on the ground of disability in the labour market can cover various aspects of employment including working conditions such as working hours, remuneration, working tasks and promotions as well as aspects like recruitment and dismissal.[138]

The Committee on the Convention on the Rights of Persons with Disabilities, in its concluding observations, has highlighted the difficulties faced by persons with disabilities in some countries. In China's report, the Committee raised concerns about the high unemployment rate of persons with disabilities as well as their average salary rank that fell well below that of persons without disabilities. The Committee recommended that China introduce affirmative action to promote employment of persons with disabilities, inter alia, to prioritise their employment as civil servants.[139]

An example of affirmative action on the national level through legislative and policy measures is the Tanzanian Persons with Disabilities Act.[140] This legislation provides a specific obligation for employers, public or private, to give priority to persons with disabilities in vacant posts where such persons meet the minimum qualifications for employment. In addition, it obligates the Minister to make regulations requiring every employer with a workforce of twenty and above to employ persons with disabilities based on a quota system and ensure that three percent (3%) of this force constitutes of persons with disabilities.[141]

---

138 Maria Ventegodt Liisberg, "Art. 27 [Work and Employment]" in Vallentina Della Fina et al. (eds.) *The United Nations Convention on the Rights of Persons with Disabilities: A Commentary* (Cham: Springer, 2017), 503.

139 Committee on the Rights of Persons with Disabilities, Concluding Observations on the Initial Report of China, 8th session, September 2012, UN doc. CRPD/C/CHN/CO/1, paras. 77 and 78.

140 United Republic of Tanzania, Act No. 9 of 2010.

141 *Id.* at Sec. 31(1–2).

Conclusion

The right to non-discrimination is a fundamental principle of international human rights law. This chapter has analysed how this right/principle cuts across and has been incorporated in various international human rights instruments. This principle has also been interpreted by the treaties' respective monitoring bodies/committees in various contexts of rights such as economic, social, civil, political and cultural rights and still holds ground as a common principle in all the international human rights systems.

Part 2: Non-Discrimination at Work: The ILO

The move towards international labour law instruments can be traced as early as the beginning of the 19th century. Though some argue that international labour law is as old as labour itself,[142] this may be seen an exaggeration, especially when the notion of labour is then interpreted broadly as to include, for example, agricultural work.[143] The development of international labour law is however tightly intertwined with the advent of industrialization.[144]

At the time of the creation of the ILO in 1919 as part of the Treaty of Versailles after the First World War, international labour law was considered urgently necessary. This is because at the time, human activity was largely structured around war and work, both of which had become global.[145] The former was dealt with through the creation of the League of Nations while the latter was dealt with through the creation of the ILO. Thus, to remedy widespread social unrest, the ILO was created to promote social progress and overcome social and economic conflicts of interests through dialogue and cooperation,[146] whilst declaring that "universal and lasting peace can be established only if it is based on social justice".[147] The reasoning behind the need for international labour law thus focused strongly on issues of social justice and consolidation of peace.[148] After World War II, the principle that "labour is not a commodity",

142 Nicolas Valticos, *International Labour* (The Netherlands: Springer, 2013) 17.

143 Martin Vranken, *Death of Labour Law? Comparative Perspectives* (Victoria: Melbourne University Press, 2009), 142.

144 *Id.*

145 Lee Swepston et al. *The ILO and the Quest for Social Justice* (Geneva: ILO, 2009), 2.

146 *Id.*

147 Constitution of the International Labour Organisation, 1919.

148 Valticos, supra note 142.

which was part of the Declaration of Philadelphia,[149] became part of the ILO constitution.

Labour rights were subsequently incorporated in various international human rights instruments such as the Universal Declaration of Human Rights (UDHR), the International Covenant on Civil and Political Rights (ICCPR), the International Covenant on Economic Social and Cultural Rights (ICESCR) and several regional instruments, in addition to the ILO instruments, making labour rights an integral part of the framework of human rights in international law. Included as labour rights, for example, are individual rights such as protections against discrimination, which might be considered individual as they apply in the workplace, but which are capable of also being effectively advanced through the collective labour rights—freedom of association and collective bargaining.[150]

Labour rights and human rights have historically developed parallel because of their different (though related) intellectual and ideological origins and because states, international bodies, social actors, and scholars have been unable or unwilling to integrate them into a single discourse.[151] Here, attention has to be drawn to the fact that labour standards were internationally acclaimed a full quarter century and a world war prior to the embodiment of human rights in the Universal Declaration.[152] Rene Cassin, the principal author of the Universal Declaration, stated in 1950 that the ILO Constitution, which was an integral part of the Treaty of Peace signed at Versailles in 1919, represented the first instance of a contractual foundation for and "international law regarding fundamental individual freedoms."[153]

Despite the incorporation of labour rights (rights at work) in various international and regional human rights treaties, there have been arguments as to whether the international labour standards as generated by the ILO have the same status and value as that of the human rights stipulated in the international human rights treaties. The conception of labour rights as human

---

149 Article 1(a), Declaration Concerning the Aims and Purposes of the International Labour Organisation, 1944.

150 Peter Barnacle, "Promoting Labour Rights in International Financial Institutions and Trade Regimes" *Saskatchewan Law Review* 67 (2004), 609.

151 *See* Harry Arthurs; "Labour Law after Labour" in Guy Davidov and Brian Langille (eds.) *The Idea of Labour Law* (Oxford: Oxford University Press, 2011), 23.

152 Nicholas Valticos, "International Labour Standards and Human Rights: Approaching the Year 2000" *International Labour Review* 137:2 (1998), 13.

153 Kofi Addo, *Core Labour Standards and International Trade: Lessons from the Regional Context* (Heidelberg: Springer, 2015), 128.

rights, or whether labour rights are or have the status of human rights, has been an issue contested by various scholars taking positions on either side of the notion. It has been argued that the "contrast between universal human rights and labour rights with respect to moral weight of the claims, their universal application, the strictness of the standards and their variability over time, create significant doubt whether labour rights are properly classified as universal human rights.[154]

Another argument that has been reiterated against the concept of "labour rights as human rights" is the universality of these rights in that they do not apply to everyone, but only to those in paid employment or in employment-like relationships.[155] This is to say that in contrast to human rights, which are universal and possessed by all human beings by virtue of their humanity, labour rights can be defined as the set of rights that humans possess by virtue of their status as workers. The particularity of this definition can also be restrictive, of course, for it limits the rights holders to their identity or function as workers, and what constitutes work is also a contested question as informal work and non-traditional forms of work have sometimes been excluded from the definition of work.[156] However, to counter this argument is the notion of universality which is argued by Macklem that "while labour rights as workers' rights operate primarily to protect the domestic rights of workers from international competition, the normative significance of labour rights in international human rights law lies in the universality of the interests they seek to protect."[157] The adoption of the Declaration on Fundamental Rights at Work, discussed below, sets out a unanimous declaration and recognition by the international community of labour rights in the core labour standards as fundamental human rights, including the right to non-discrimination.

That which is unique about the ILO is its tripartite structure in which its organs consist of representatives of governments, employers and workers, thus facilitating the creation and supervision of international labour standards in a

154 Patrick Macklem, *The Sovereignty of Human Rights* (New York: Oxford University Press, 2015). *See also* Hugh Collins, "Theories of Rights as Justifications for Labour Law" in Guy Davidov and Brian Langille (eds.) *The Idea of Labour Law* (Oxford: Oxford University Press, 2011), 143.

155 *Id.* at 142.

156 Kevin Kolben, 'Labour Rights as Human Rights?' (2010), 50 (2), *Virginia Journal of International Law* 453.

157 Patrick Macklem, "The Right to Bargain Collectively in International Law: Workers' Rights, Human Rights, International Rights?" in Philip Alston(ed.) Labour Rights as Human Rights (2005) 70.

setting where adoption of the labour standards exists with the support of components in labour relations. This is backed up by a two-tier supervisory system consisting of first, a regular system of supervision based on regular reporting by member states on how they have implemented ILO standards. Second is a special procedure which consists of procedures for complaints, representations and special complaints procedure regarding freedom of association (the Committee on Freedom of Association).[158]

The Core Labour Standards

The ILO adopted the 1998 Declaration on Fundamental Principles and Rights at Work,[159] setting forth a set of constitutional principles and rights that are universal and apply to/are binding on all States by virtue of their membership with the ILO, regardless of whether they have ratified the relevant conventions. These fundamental categories include: freedom of association and the effective recognition of the right to collective bargaining, the elimination of forced or compulsory labour, the abolition of child labour and the elimination of discrimination in respect of employment and occupation.[160] These principles are embodied in eight conventions that stipulate the specific rights associated with these principles: Freedom of Association and Protection of the Right to Organise Convention 1948 (No. 87), Right to Organise and Collective Bargaining Convention 1949 (No. 98), Forced Labour Convention 1930 (No. 29), Abolition of Forced Labour Convention 1957 (No. 105), Minimum Age Convention 1973 (No. 138), Worst Forms of Child Labour Convention 1999 (No. 182), Equal Remuneration Convention 1951 (No. 100) and Discrimination (Employment and Occupation) Convention, 1958 (No. 111).

The Declaration places an obligation on the states to respect, promote and realise, in good faith and according to the ILO Constitution and the principles concerning the fundamental rights that are subject to the core conventions.[161] The essence of the Declaration is that it has enshrined the standards that are

---

158 For further details, *see* "The ILO Supervisory System" available at website of the ILO, ilo.org.

159 Declaration on Fundamental Principles and Rights at Work, 1998, adopted by the International Labour Conference at its Eighty-sixth Session, Geneva, 18 June 1998.

160 For more details on the Declaration and its follow-up procedures, see "ILO Declaration on Fundamental Principles at Work" available at website of the ILO at ilo.org.

161 Art. 2, ILO Declaration on Fundamental Principles and Rights at Work, adopted by the International Labour Conference at its Eighty-sixth Session, Geneva, 18 June 1998.

"equivalent" to human rights[162] as well as characterised labour rights as fundamental rights at the international level.[163]

The Equal Remuneration Convention, 1951 (No. 100)

The ILO Equal Remuneration Convention is one of the fundamental eight ILO conventions that provides for non-discrimination at work, and more specifically, equality of pay on basis of the principle of "equal remuneration for work of equal value" affirmed in the ILO Constitution.[164] This principle means that rates and types of remuneration should be based not on an employee's sex, but on an objective evaluation of the work performed.[165] Historically there have been different reasons for the difference in earnings between men and women. These include classifications at lower levels of jobs done by the majority of women, differences in skills, qualifications, seniority and sectors of employment, concentration of women in flexible work such as part time, piece rate or temporary work, all of which are poorly paid.[166] Convention No. 100, by guaranteeing equal pay for work of equal value, opens the door for examination of structural gender biases in the labour market.[167]

Convention No. 100 defines the term *remuneration* as including the ordinary, basic or minimum wage or salary and any additional emoluments whatsoever payable directly or indirectly, whether in cash or in kind, by the employer to the worker and arising out of the worker's employment. The Committee of Experts on the Application of Conventions and Recommendations (CEACR) has given a broad definition of remuneration, which includes not only "the ordinary, basic or minimum wage or salary", but also "any additional emoluments whatsoever payable directly or indirectly, whether in cash or in kind" and covers all the emoluments workers may receive in exchange for their labour, including additional benefits in kind, to which a monetary value may be attributed. Accordingly, any exclusion from remuneration of components such as compensation for extra duties, refunds of expenses, accommodation,

162 Hans Michael Wolffgand and Wolfram Peuerhake, "The Necessity for Incorporation of Core Labour Standards in the World Trade Organisation" *36 Journal of World Trade* (2002), 883, 890.

163 *See* Judy Fudge, "The New Discourse of Labour Rights: From Social to Fundamental?" 29:1 *Comparative Labour Law and Policy Journal* (2007), 1–2.

164 Preamble, Constitution of the International Labour Organisation, 1919.

165 International Labour Office, ABC of Women Workers' Rights and Gender Equality, 1st Edition (Geneva: International Labour Organisation, 2000), 38.

166 *Id.*

167 International Labour Office, ABC of Women Workers' Rights and Gender Equality, 2nd Edition (Geneva: International Labour Organisation, 2007), 8.

travel allowances, bonuses, rewards and family allowances is inconsistent with Article 1(a) of the Convention.[168] Again, the term *equal remuneration for men and women workers for work of equal value* are rates of remuneration established without discrimination based on sex.[169]

The Convention obliges the Members to ensure and promote the application to all workers of the principle of equal remuneration for men and women workers for work of equal value and to and use appropriate methods for determining rates of remuneration.[170] The Convention provides for the various ways in which this principle can be applied, including through national laws or regulations, legally established or recognised machinery for wage determination, collective agreements between employers and workers or a combination of the various means.[171] Although the methods to be followed in objective appraisal of jobs are to be decided the authorities responsible for the determination of rates of remuneration,[172] the Member states have the responsibility to promote objective appraisal of jobs on basis of the work to be performed.[173] Interesting is the case of Malaysia, where the government stated in its report that rates of remuneration are determined through market forces, the minimum wage legislation and collective bargaining and that the government gives effect to the principle of equal remuneration set forth in the Convention by ensuring that men and women are paid equally "for the same job" as well as periodic inspections at workplaces. The Committee, while highlighting the continuing gender wage gap in various occupations, concluded that the concept of "work of equal value" in the Convention allows a broad scope of comparison going beyond equal remuneration for "equal", "the same", or "similar" work, and encompasses work that is of an entirely different nature, but which is of nevertheless of equal value.[174] The Convention also provides for situations that do not contradict the principle of equal remuneration for men and women workers for work of equal value. This includes differential rates between

168 Direct Request (CEACR)-adopted 2015, Published 105th ILC session (2016), Equal Remuneration Convention (No. 100), 1951 on Angola.

169 Art. 1, Equal Remuneration Convention No. 100, 1951.

170 *Id.* at Art. 1.

171 *Id.* at Art. 2.

172 *Id.* at Art. 3(2.).

173 *Id.* at Art. 3(1).

174 Observation (CEACR)-adopted 2014, published 104th ILC session (2015) Equal Remuneration Convention, 1951 (No. 100)-Malaysia. *See also* Direct Request (CEACR)-adopted 2015, published 105th ILC session (2016) Equal Remuneration Convention, 1951 (No. 100)-Eritrea; Direct Request (CEACR)-adopted 2015, published 105th ILC session (2016) Equal Remuneration Convention, 1951-Bahamas.

workers that correspond, without regard to sex, to differences as determined by such objective appraisal in the work to be performed.[175] Finally, reiterating the ILO's tripartite nature, the Convention requires that members cooperate with employers' and workers' organisations concerned in order to give effect to the provisions of the Convention.[176]

The Discrimination (Employment and Occupation) Convention, 1958 (No. 111)

Equality of opportunity and treatment has been one of the objectives of the ILO since its foundation.[177] The principle was recognised in Article 41 (2) of the original ILO constitution and was restated by the ILC in the in the Declaration of Philadelphia concerning the aims and objectives of the ILO, stating:

> All human beings irrespective of race, creed or sex, have the right to pursue both their material well-being and their spiritual developments in conditions of freedom and dignity, of economic security and equal opportunity.[178]

The preamble to the Convention lays down the ILO's vision in adopting Convention No. 111 by referring to not only the right to non-discrimination under the Declaration of Philadelphia (as previously quoted), but also that discrimination constitutes a violation of rights enunciated in the UDHR. This Convention defines discrimination as including any distinction, exclusion or preference made on the basis of race, colour, sex, religion, political opinion, national extraction or social origin, which has the effect of nullifying or impairing equality of opportunity or treatment in employment or occupation.[179] The Convention does not limit the grounds of discrimination to the ones in this clause, but allows Members to identify other grounds of discrimination that have the same effect on equality of opportunity and treatment, but after consultation with representative employers' and workers' organisations, where such exist, and with other appropriate bodies.[180] This section displays the

175 Art. 3(3), Equal Remuneration Convention No. 100, 1951.

176 *Id.* at Art. 4.

177 *See* Henrik Karl Nielsen, "The Concept of Discrimination in ILO Convention No. 111", The International and Comparative Law Quarterly (1994), 827, 856.

178 Sec. II(a), ILO Declaration of Philadelphia: Declaration Concerning the Aims and Purposes of the International Labour Organisation, 1944.

179 Art. 1(1)(a), Convention No. 111, 1958.

180 *Id.* at Art. 1(1)(b).

non-exhaustive nature of the list of grounds of discrimination provided for in Article 1(1)(a) of the Convention, similar to the ICCPR and the ICESCR. Again similar to the HRC and the CESCR, the CEACR in interpreting this section has set forth such additional grounds of discrimination including disability and HIV status.[181]

Convention No. 111 also provides for a wide interpretation of the terms "employment" and "occupation" to include access to vocational training, access to employment and to particular occupations, and terms and conditions of employment.[182] It also places obligations on the members, which include declaring and pursuing a national policy designed to promote, by methods appropriate to national conditions and practice, equality of opportunity and treatment in respect of employment and occupation, with a view to eliminating any discrimination in respect thereof.[183] Pursuant to this national policy, the convention requires members, by methods appropriate to national conditions and practice, to seek the co-operation of employers' and workers' organisations and other appropriate bodies in promoting the acceptance and observance of this policy. Members are to enact legislation and promote educational programmes as may be calculated to secure the acceptance and observance of the policy. Members are to repeal any statutory provisions and modify any administrative instructions or practices that are inconsistent with the policy and pursue the policy in respect of employment under the direct control of a national authority. Members are to ensure observance of the policy in the activities of vocational guidance, vocational training and placement services under the direction of a national authority and lastly to indicate in its annual reports on the application of the Convention the action taken in pursuance of the policy and the results secured by such action.[184]

Members, after consulting employers' and workers' organisations, may determine other special measures required for persons who, on grounds such as sex, age, disablement, family responsibility, social or cultural status, require such protection or assistance.[185] For example, the CEACR has provided for the

181 Direct Request (CEACR)-adopted 2015, published 105th ILC session (2016), Discrimination (Employment and Occupation) Convention, 1958 (No. 111)-Chad. The Committee provided for the additional grounds of discrimination by emphasizing on the protection of rights of persons living with HIV and AIDS as well as the protection of rights of persons with disabilities.

182 *Id.* at Art. 1(3).

183 *Id.* at Art. 2.

184 *Id.* at Art. 3.

185 *Id.* at Art. 5(2).

importance of special measures in promoting effective equality of persons belonging to national minorities.[186] Again, in the case of South Africa, the Committee required the government to provide information on the affirmative action measures taken by employers to address discrimination against black people, women and people with disabilities, pursuant to the country's Employment Equity Act (EEA).[187]

The Convention also provides for situations that do not amount to discrimination. First is distinction, exclusion or preference in respect of a particular job based on the inherent requirements thereof.[188] This includes, for example, exclusion in certain jobs of young persons (14 to 18 years of age) and pregnant women.[189] Second, similar to the human rights treaties discussed herein, is the application of special measures of protection or assistance that originate from other ILO conventions or recommendations.[190] The Committee of Experts has found that this includes measures to protect women, indigenous populations, disabled and aged persons.[191]

Conclusion

Non-discrimination is one of the core principles in the ILO system, as it is in the international human rights system. The two systems are part of the general international human rights framework. The interpretations of these rights by the ILO bodies/Committees are quite similar to the interpretations by the monitoring bodies of the international human rights treaties discussed in the previous chapter. All these instruments and bodies put together create a coherent system of human rights. This complementary feature is evidenced in a number of ways. First is the compatibility clauses found in the various human rights treaties referring to other human rights treaties.[192] Additionally is the reference, by the monitoring committees, to the reports and observations

186 Observation (CEACR)-adopted 2007, published 97th ILC session (2008) Discrimination (Employment and Occupation) Convention, 1958 (No. 111)-Slovakia, para. 2.

187 Direct Request (CEACR)-adopted 2011, published 101st ILC session (2012) Discrimination (Employment and Occupation) Convention (No. 111), 1958-South Africa.

188 *Id.* at Art. 1(2).

189 Direct Request (CEACR)-adopted 2002, published 91st ILC session (2003), Discrimination (Employment and Occupation) Convention, 1958 (No. 111)-Benin.

190 *Id.* at Art. 5(1).

191 International Labour Conference, Equality in Employment and Occupation: General Survey by the Committee of Experts on the Application of Conventions and Recommendations (1988), paras. 148–158.

192 For example, both Art. 22(2) of the ICCPR and Art. 8(3) of the ICESCR refer to ILO Conventions as the applicable standards.

of other committees. For example, the ILO's CEACR frequently refers to the observations and conclusions of other international human rights treaties' monitoring bodies such as the CtEDAW,[193] the HRC,[194] the CERD[195] and the CESCR.[196] Though labour rights have historically been contested as not being human rights, the most recent international instruments evidently recognize labour rights as human rights.

Part 3: Non-Discrimination and International Human Rights Protections: Regional Avenues

Introduction

Human rights have not only been incorporated in various international public law instruments, but also in regional treaties and other instruments. The significance of the regional treaties lies in the fact that they play an important role in the promotion of international human rights standards. What is unique to the regional instruments is that as countries in a region have shared customs, values, cultures and practices and also similar political, economic and social concerns, the regional human rights treaties localise international human rights standards in view of these region-specific concerns. This is to say that the regional human rights treaties are closer in norms to their respective local populations. Although there are numerous regional human rights treaties and monitoring mechanisms, this chapter will focus on the three oldest and most established regions; the Council of Europe, the Organisation of American States and the African Union (formerly the Organisation of African Unity).

The Council of Europe

The Council of Europe was established after World War II with the aim of safeguarding and realising the principles of human rights, political liberty, the rule of law and democracy by the Member States, in unity, for economic and

193 Direct Request (CEACR)-adopted 2011, published 101st session (2012) Equal Remuneration Convention, 1951 (No. 100)-Kyrgyzstan.

194 Observation (CEACR)-adopted 2013, published 103rd ILC session (2014) Discrimination (Employment and Occupation) Convention, 1958 (No. 111)-Germany.

195 Direct Request (CEACR)-adopted 2010, published 100th ILC session (2011) Discrimination (Employment and Occupation) Convention, 1958-Cambodia.

196 Observation (CEACR)-adopted 2010, published 100th ILC session (2011) Equal Remuneration Convention, 1951 (No. 100)-Philippines.

social progress.[197] The Member States adopted the 1948 European Convention on Human Rights (ECHR), which reiterates these same principles,[198] to help achieve these aims.

The European Convention on Human Rights

Having been adopted before the international twin covenants of 1966, ICESCR and ICCPR, the ECHR was the first of the regional as well as international human rights treaties adopted after and drawing from the United Nations Universal Declaration of Human Rights. The Convention's preamble lays down the principles of human rights and fundamental freedoms, political democracy and the rule of law. The preamble also puts forth consideration of the UDHR. It denotes its aim to "take the first steps for the collective enforcement of certain of the rights stated in the UDHR".[199]

When it comes to the right to non-discrimination, the Article 14 ECHR states:

> The enjoyment of the rights and freedoms set forth in this Convention shall be secured without discrimination on any ground such as sex, race, colour, language, religion, political or other opinion, national or social origin, association with a national minority, property, birth or other status.

One must note early on that the Convention does not contain a definition of discrimination. However, Bruun argues that the Court applies a consolidated methodology by way of systematic reference to international standards and the case law of their respective supervisory bodies.[200]

Several crucial features detected in the wording of the provision further explain the status as well as scope of the right itself. First, Article 14 is "parasitic" or does not have "independent existence" as it has effect solely in relation to the "enjoyment of the rights and freedoms" safeguarded by this provision, although it is not necessary to show that there has been a breach of another provision in the Convention.[201] Again, the provision prohibits discrimination

---

197 *See* Preamble and Art. 1, Statute of the Council of Europe, 1949.

198 *See* Preamble, European Convention on Human Rights, 1950.

199 *Id.*

200 For further details on this methodology and case references see Niklas Bruun, "Prohibition of Discrimination under Art. 14 of the European Convention on Human Rights" in Filip Dorssemont, et al. (eds.) *The European Convention on Human Rights and the Employment Relation* (Oxford: Hart Publishing, 2013), 372.

201 *Id.*, at 371. *See also Sommerfeld v Germany*, ECtHR (Grand Chamber), App No. 31871/96, 8th July 2003.

in the enjoyment of the rights set forth in the Convention, limiting the scope of the article to such rights. However, Article 1 of Protocol 12 extends the protection against discrimination to all rights set forth by law,[202] meaning even national law. Therefore, the meaning of discrimination in the Convention (art. 14) and in the Protocol is identical, with the difference being only in the scope of their application.[203] This is to say that the two provisions together are analogous to Articles 2(1) and 26 of the ICCPR respectively.

Another feature is the non-exhaustive list of the grounds of discrimination in Article 14 ECHR. Here, the phrase "any other status" shows that the provision is "an open-model non-discrimination clause"[204] which is not limited to an exhaustive list of discrimination grounds. In addition, it has been argued that the clause "on grounds such as" means that the provision mentions the various grounds as examples while perhaps the drafters had considered these grounds to constitute the most problematic ones.[205] Corroborating this position is the application of the article by the European Court on Human Rights (ECtHR), which has applied grounds of discrimination not listed in the Convention, such as discrimination based on birth out-of-wedlock.[206]

Coming to the issue of positive or affirmative actions, the Convention does not include any provision on this, as do the ICCPR and ICESCR. However, the Preamble to Protocol No. 12 states that, "the principle of non-discrimination does not prevent state parties from taking measures in order to promote full and effective equality, provided that there is an objective and reasonable justification for those measures." Further elaborating this stance is an explanatory report of Protocol No. 12, which states that:

> The fact that there are certain groups or categories of persons who are disadvantaged, or the existence of de facto inequalities, may constitute justifications for adopting measures providing for specific advantages in order to promote equality, provided that the proportionality principle is respected … However, the present Protocol does not impose any obligation to adopt such measures. Such a programmatic obligation would sit

202 Council of Europe, Protocol No. 12 to the European Convention on Human Rights, 2000.

203 ECtHR, *Sejdic Finci v Bosnia-Herzegovina*, App No. 27996/06, 22nd December 2009.

204 Oddný Mjöll Arnardóttir, "Non-Discrimination under Art. 14 ECHR: The Burden of Proof" *Scandinavian Studies in Law* (2007), 14.

205 Janneke Gerards, "The Discrimination Grounds of Art. 14 of the European Convention on Human Rights" 13:1 *Human Rights Law Review* (2013), 104.

206 ECtHR, *Mazurek v France*, Appl. No. 34406/97, 1st February 2000; ECtHR (Grand Chamber), *Christine Goodwin v the United Kingdom*, Appl. No. 28957/95, 11th July 2002.

> ill with the whole nature of the Convention and its control system which are based on the collective guarantee of individual rights which are formulated in terms sufficiently specific to be justifiable.[207]

Thus, affirmative action is not contrary to the Convention, as long as the consequent differential treatment is objectively and reasonably justified, that is, pursues a legitimate aim and it does not pursue this aim by disproportionate means.[208]

Discrimination in Employment: The European Social Charter

The 1961 European Social Charter (ESC) was adopted as a complement of economic and social rights to the European Convention on Human Rights. It thus contains fundamental social rights of workers. The adoption of the 1988 Protocol expanded the rights in the Charter. Revision of the Charter in 1996 further expanded the list of rights covered by the Charter.[209]

The Charter contains a general clause on non-discrimination in the enjoyment of the rights in the Charter:

> The enjoyment of the rights set forth in this Charter shall be secured without discrimination on any ground such as race, colour, sex, language, religion, political or other opinion, national extraction or social origin, health, association with a national minority, birth or other status.[210]

This provision is similar to that found in the ECHR and has similar features, including the non-exhaustive element discussed earlier. Coming to the issue of discrimination in employment, Article 20 on the right to equal treatment in matters of employment and occupation without discrimination on the ground of sex provides that:

---

207 Explanatory Report of Protocol No. 12 to the Convention for the Protection of Human Rights and Fundamental Freedoms, 29(16), August 2000.

208 Olivier De Schutter, The Prohibition of Discrimination under European Human Rights Law: Relevance for EU Racial and Employment Equality Directives (Luxemburg: European Communities, 2005), 19.

209 The 1996 Revised Charter is a separate treaty from the original 1961 Charter and does not amend or replace the latter. Once a State party to the original 1961 Charter accedes the revised 1996 Charter, the latter includes the obligations under the former.

210 Art. E, European Social Charter, 1961.

> With a view to ensuring the effective exercise of the right to equal opportunities and equal treatment in matters of employment and occupation without discrimination on the grounds of sex, the Parties undertake to recognise that right and to take appropriate measures to ensure or promote its application in the following fields:
>
> a access to employment, protection against dismissal and occupational reintegration;
> b vocational guidance, training, retraining and rehabilitation;
> c terms of employment and working conditions, including remuneration;
> d career development, including promotion.

Another provision relevant to non-discrimination in employment is that on the right of men and women workers to equal pay for work of equal value.[211] The original 1961 Charter did not have equality between men and women as a human rights principle. The two provisions, Articles 20 and 4(3) overlap in that equal pay for equal value of work is regarded as an aspect of the right to equal opportunities in employment.[212]

The elaboration and conclusions of the European Committee of Social Rights (ECSR)[213] are somewhat similar to those of the ILO bodies discussed previously. For example, the Committee has concluded that the principle of equality applies to all the elements of remuneration, including benefits.[214]

The Charter sets forth certain situations that are not considered as discrimination. First is the protection of pregnant women, confinement and postnatal period.[215] Second is occupational activities that due to their nature or the context in which they are carried out, can be entrusted only to persons of a particular sex.[216] Last is the adoption of specific measures aimed at removing *de facto* inequalities.[217] It is important to note that all of these exceptions are provided for in the ILO Convention No. 111 as discussed above in Chapter Two.

---

211 Art. 4(3), European Social Charter, 1961, rev.

212 *See* Zoe Adams and Simon Deakin, "The Right to a Fair Remuneration" in Klaus Lörcher et al. *The European Social Charter and the Employment Relation* (Portland: Hart Publishing, 2017), 213.

213 The ECSR's function is to deliberate on the national reports of Member States and rule as to their conformity with the ESC and adopt conclusions thereof.

214 ECSR, Conclusion I, Statement of Interpretation on Art. 4(3) (1969).

215 ESC, Appendix to the Revised ESC, Art. 20(2).

216 *Id.* at Art. 20(4).

217 *Id.* at Art. 20(3).

The Organisation of African Unity/The African Union

The Organisation of African Unity (OAU) was established in 1963 upon adoption of its Charter. With one of the primary functions of the organization being to eradicate colonialism and establishing independence of African nations,[218] the Charter reflects the principles that were of concern to these African states at that time. Such principles include the inalienable right of all people to control their own destiny (self-determination), the responsibility to harness natural and human resources for advancement of the people, safeguarding of independence, sovereignty and territorial integrity and fight against neo-colonialism in all its forms.[219] The Charter also affirms adherence to the UN Charter and the UDHR as the "solid foundation" of the OAU, and sets forth the essential objectives of freedom, equality, justice and dignity.[220] The purposes of the Unity include promoting international cooperation with due regard to the UN Charter and the UDHR.[221] One crucial aspect of the Charter is that there is no mention of human rights in the principles and purposes of the Charter, save for when it refers to the UDHR. This shows a focus of the Charter on the protection of the state and not people.[222] The adoption of the African Charter on Human and Peoples' Rights in 1981 and its coming into force in 1985 introduced human rights into the OAU system.

The OAU transformed into the African Union (AU) in 2001 after the coming into force of the Constitutive Act of the Union, which replaced the OAU charter. This Act, as opposed to its predecessor, is based on the principle of human rights, among others, where states are "determined to promote and protect human and peoples' rights, consolidate democratic institutions and culture and to ensure good governance and the rule of law."[223] The Act also takes due account of the UN Charter and the UDHR as well as promotes and protects human and peoples' rights in accordance with the ACHPR and other relevant human rights instruments.[224] The Act also explicitly sets forth the principles of the AU, including respect for democratic principles, human rights, the rule of

218 Corinne Packer and Donald Rukare, "The New African Union and Its Constitutive Act" 96:2 *American Journal of International Law* (2002), 366.

219 *See* Preamble, OAU Charter, 1963.

220 *Id.*

221 Art. II(e), OAU Charter, 1963.

222 For a more detailed discussion, *see* Rachel Murray, *Human Rights in Africa: From the OAU to the African Union* (New York: Cambridge University Press, 2004), 7.

223 Preamble, Constitutive Act of the African Union, 2000.

224 Art. 3(e) and 3(h), Constitutive Act of the African Union, 2000.

law and good governance[225] and the promotion of gender equality.[226] Despite this positive departure of the Act from its predecessor on the matter of human rights, it has maintained the latter's position on the defence of sovereignty and territorial integrity[227] as well as non-interference by any Member State in the internal affairs of another.[228]

The African Charter on Human and Peoples' Rights

The 1981 African Charter on Human and Peoples' Rights (ACHPR) was adopted after discussions in several avenues had taken place pointing at the importance of a regional human rights instrument in Africa.[229] The charter itself contains all three generations of rights, that is civil and political, economic, social and cultural as well as collective/peoples' rights.

Before discussing the content of the Charter in relation to non-discrimination protections, it is necessary to highlight the overall context in which this instrument was conceived. The 1980's was a crucial period in this region because it was a period characterized by the rise of independent states and the desire of an instrument that would provide a somewhat "African identity" in encompassing international standards of human rights. Here, the Charter's preamble provides insight. First, the preamble speaks of the total liberalisation of Africa and elimination of colonialism, neo-colonialism, apartheid, Zionism as well as dismantling of all forms of discrimination.[230] Naturally, in all the forms of domination mentioned in this preamble, discrimination was central to such regimes, particularly and the desire of the founders of the Charters to eliminate this discrimination is apparent. That which is interesting is the Charter's perception of the virtues of African historical traditions as well as the values of African civilisation which should inspire and characterize their reflection on

225 Art. 4(m), Constitutive Act of the African Union, 2000.

226 *Id.* at Art. 4(l).

227 *Id.* at Art. 3(b).

228 *Id.* at Art. 4(g).

229 The International Association of Jurists held an African Conference on the Rule of Law (3–7 January 1961) where African Lawyers made a proposal that an African convention for the protection of human rights, which would fit into an international system for the protection of human rights, be drafted. See *International Commission of Jurists, African Conference on the Rule of Law: A Report on the Proceedings of the Conference, Geneva, 1961*, 6; See also *United Nations Seminar on the Establishment of Regional Commissions on Human Rights with Special Reference to Africa*, 10–21 September 1979.

230 *See* Preamble, African Charter of Human and Peoples' Rights (herein after the Charter) 1981.

the concept of human and peoples' rights. These reflect the Charter's inspiration by African legal philosophy desires and needs.[231]

The Charter acknowledges the state members' affirmation in the adherence of principles of human rights and freedoms contained in the UDHR, international declarations, conventions and other types of instruments adopted by the Union and United Nations.[232] It is crucial to note that at the time of adoption of the UDHR by the UNGA, only four African countries were not under foreign rule and were members of the UN. Of these four, Egypt, Ethiopia and Liberia voted in favour of the Declaration while South Africa, which at the time was under apartheid rule, abstained from voting.[233] Therefore, in relation to the need for an African human rights instrument, a view of concern was that the principles expressed in the UNGA did not necessarily reflect African values or problems embodied in peculiarly African solutions.[234] One unique feature of the Charter is the notion of peoples' rights, which is an embodiment of the African conception and philosophy of a person in society where one is not regarded on an "isolated and abstract individual, but an integral member of a group animated by a spirit of solidarity."[235] The OAU's Rapporteur's report also confirms this perception.[236]

Coming to non-discrimination protections under the Charter, first and foremost, the Charter places an obligation on the contracting States to "recognise the rights, duties and freedoms enshrined in the Charter and to provide for their effectiveness within their territory through legislation or other domestic

231 Daniel Turack, "The African Charter on Human and Peoples' Rights: Some Preliminary Thoughts", 17:3 *Akron Law Review* (1984), 378.

232 Preamble, Charter, 1981.

233 For further details see Hilary Charlesworth, "Universal Declaration of Human Rights (1948)", Oxford Public International Law, Max Plank Encyclopedia of Public International Law (MPEPIL), Oxford University Press, 2015.

234 Richard Gittleman, "The African Charter on Human and Peoples' Rights: A Legal Analysis", 22:4 *Virginia Journal of International Law* (1982), 671. *See also* Seminar on the Regional Commissions on Human Rights with Special Reference to Africa, U.N. Doc ST/TAO/HR/39 (1969), Cairo, 2–15 September 1969.

235 Richard N. Kiwanuka, "The Meaning of 'People' in the African Charter on Human and Peoples' Rights" 82:1 *American Journal of International Law* (1988), 80–101, 82.

236 The Rapporteur's report stated that "Noting that in Africa, Man is part and parcel of the group, some delegations concluded that individual rights could be explained and justified only by the rights of the community. Consequently, they wished that the Draft Charter made room for the Peoples' Rights and adopted a more balanced approach to economic, social and cultural rights on the one hand and political and civil rights on the other," *see* Rapporteur's Report, OAU Doc. CM/1149 (XXXVII), 4 para. 13.

measures".[237] The right granting freedom from discrimination in the Charter is generally provided for under Article 2, which states that:

> Every individual shall be entitled to the enjoyment of the rights and freedoms recognised and guaranteed in the present Charter without distinction of any kind such as race, ethnic group, colour, sex, language, religion, political or any other opinion, national and social origin, fortune, birth or any status.

The list of discriminatory grounds is not exhaustive and "any status" has been interpreted to mean other grounds not explicitly stipulated in the clause.[238] The African Commission on Human Rights has recently expanded this list by providing for additional grounds such as sexual orientation, gender identity, disability, health status, economic or indigenous status, etc.[239]

This provision also makes the Charter unique because the other (regional) instruments, that is, the American Convention and the European Convention, do not have ethnicity as a ground for discrimination.[240] Again, this reflects the African principles under the OAU Charter, referring to the promotion of "understanding among our peoples ... in a larger unity transcending ethnic and national differences."[241] The importance of the ground of ethnicity in the African context can be viewed in a number of ways. First is a tradition of favouritism.[242] Unequal treatment of citizens on the basis of ethnicity is not a new issue in the African context, where ethnic bias is a product of personalised

237 Art. 1, African Charter.

238 *See* African Commission on Human and Peoples' Rights, Principles and Guideline on the Implementation of Economic, Social and Cultural Rights in the African Charter on Human and Peoples' Rights, para. 19 African Commission on Human and Peoples' Rights, General Comment No. 4 on the African Charter on Human and Peoples' Rights: The Right to Redress for Victims of Torture and Other Cruel and Inhuman or Degrading Punishment or Treatment (Art. 5), 21st Extra-Ordinary session, 4th March 2017, para. 20.

239 African Commission on Human and Peoples' Rights, General Comment No. 4 on the African Charter on Human and Peoples' Rights: The Right to Redress for Victims of Torture and Other Cruel and Inhuman or Degrading Punishment or Treatment (Art. 5), 21st Extra-Ordinary session, 4th March 2017, para. 20.

240 Except for the CERD and CRC, the other international human rights treaties do not have ethnicity as a ground of discrimination in their provisions.

241 Preamble, OAU Charter, cl. 4.

242 See Richard Gittleman, "The African Charter", 683; Godpower O. Okereke, "Challenges Facing Sub-Saharan Africa: The Problem of Governance" 2.2 International Journal of Social Science and Business (2017), 10.

ties, therefore, ethnic bias has features of favouritism and even corruption.[243] Here, the behaviour of leadership or government towards others/citizens varies depending on whether they are from the in-group, usually the same ethnic group.[244] This can go as far as barring distinct portions of the population from taking part in government.[245] In such cases, the express prohibition against ethnic discrimination is an important guard for fair treatment of those who are not kinsman of those in power. Second is the ethnic discrimination that has been a source of conflict in many African countries. Examples of countries that have faced civil strife due to ethnicity include Rwanda, Nigeria and Sudan, to mention but a few.

The African Commission on Human Rights was established to oversee the implementation of the Charter. The first function of the Commission is to promote human and peoples' rights by collecting documents, undertaking studies and research on African problems in the field of human and peoples' rights, as well as dissemination of information through conferences as well as the involvement in these activities of African and international institutions concerned with human rights.[246] The second function is to ensure the protection of human and peoples' rights under conditions laid down by the Charter. Last is the interpretive function. With regards to the latter, the Charter directs the consideration of other human rights instruments. In describing this function, the Charter names this as the interpretation of the provisions of the Charter at the request of a State party, an institution of the OAU or an African organisation recognised by the OAU.[247] Interesting is the provision that the Commission is to "draw inspiration from international law on human and peoples' rights, particularly from the provisions of various African instruments on Human and Peoples' Rights, the Charter of the United Nations, the Charter of the Organisation of African Unity, the Universal Declaration of Human Rights, other instruments adopted by the United Nations and by African countries in the field of Human and Peoples' Rights, as well as from the provisions

243 Richard Ilorah, "Ethnic Bias, Favouratism and Development in Africa", 26:5 *Development Southern Africa* (2009), 695–707, 696.

244 *Id.*

245 *See* Patrick Glen, "Institutionalising Democracy in Africa: A Comment on the African Charter on Democracy, Elections and Governance", 5 African Journal of Legal Studies (2012), 149–175, 174.

246 Art. 45(1).

247 Art. 45(3), ACHPR.

of various instruments adopted within the Specialised Agencies of the United Nations of which the Parties to the present Charter are members."[248]

An inadequacy of the Commission is that it is not a judicial body and can only make recommendations that can be and often are ignored by governments. This lack of an effective enforcement mechanism led to calls for the establishment of the African Court of Human and Peoples' Rights in 1998, when a Protocol to the Charter was adopted.[249] The Protocol came into force in 2004. The relationship between the Commission and the Court is a complementary one where the Court's mandate complements the protective mandate of the Commission.[250] As is the case of the Commission, the Court is also to apply the provisions of the Charter and any other relevant human rights instruments ratified by the States concerned.[251]

One of the recurring criticisms of the African Charter has focused on the "claw-back" clauses, which basically entitle a state to restrict the rights to the extent permitted by domestic law.[252] This is not to be confused with derogation clauses, which restrict a state's conduct by limiting the circumstances in which derogation may occur as well as defining those rights that are non-derogable and must be respected. These claw-back clauses become more of a challenge due to the fact that the ACHPR does not contain a general derogation clause. However, as stated earlier, the Charter does make reference to other international human rights treaties as an important aspect in interpretation of the rights in the Charter.

Discrimination in Employment

Article 15 of the ACHPR states,

> Every individual shall have the right to work under equitable and satisfactory conditions, and shall receive equal pay for equal work.

---

248 Art. 60, ACHPR.

249 Art. 1, Protocol to the African Charter on Human and Peoples' Rights on the Establishment of an African Court on Human and Peoples' Rights, 1998.

250 *Id.* at Art. 2.

251 *Id.* at Art. 7.

252 *See* Makau wa Mutua, "The African System in a Comparative Perspective", 3 *Review on the African Commission on Human and Peoples' Rights* (1993), 7; Loveness Mapura, "Negating the Promotion of Human Rights through "Claw-Back" Clauses in the African Charter on Human and Peoples' Rights" 51 *International Affairs and Global Strategy* (2016).

Although this provision provides for the right to work under "equitable and satisfactory" conditions, it is quite vague as it does not give further elaboration as to what these conditions are. It also requires "equal pay for equal work". In essence, this means, for example, that women may not face discrimination at work by being paid less than men doing the same job. However, the ILO has warned of the weakness of the use of "equal work" instead of "work of equal value" as the former applies to work that is similar (particularly in terms of task) while the latter covers work/tasks that may be different, but are of equal value, pay equity.[253]

The African Charter on the Rights and Welfare of the Child, 1990

The right to non-discrimination has also been incorporated in other specialized instruments in the region. The African Charter on the Rights and Welfare of the Child (ACRWC) is the only region-specific child rights instrument. The Charter reflects the critical situation of African children due to the unique factors of their socio-economic, cultural, traditional and developmental circumstances such as armed conflicts, exploitation etc.[254] It also reaffirms adherence to the CRC and the Declaration on the Rights and Welfare of the African Child.[255]

As for non-discrimination, it states:

> Every child shall be entitled to the enjoyment of the rights and freedoms recognized and guaranteed in this Charter irrespective of the child's or his/her parents' or legal guardians' race, ethnic group, colour, sex, language, religion, political or other opinion, national and social origin, fortune, birth or other status.[256]

This provision is similar to that of the CRC, the differences being the absence of the ground of disability and the use of the ground of fortune in the Charter, which can be analogous to property in the CRC. The Charter also provides for special measures for children with disabilities and requires the Member States to ensure effective access to various activities such as training, employment and recreation as well as reasonable accommodation for children with

253 *See* Chapter 2 above.

254 Preamble, African Charter on the Rights and Welfare of the Child, 1990.

255 *Id.*

256 *Id.* at Art. 3.

disabilities,[257] while, like the CRC, basing these obligations on progressive realisation.[258] The Charter, like the CRC sets forth its principles to be non-discrimination and the best interest of the child, which is to be the primary consideration in all actions concerning the child.[259]

Protocol to the ACHPR on the Rights of Women in Africa 2003

One of the principles of the Protocol on the Rights of women is non-discrimination as stipulated by Articles 2 and 18 ACHPR as well as international instruments such as the UDHR, ICCPR, ICESCR, and CEDAW in the light of Articles 60 and 61 ACHPR. These articles recognize regional and international human rights instruments as important reference points in application and interpretation of the Charter. The Protocol defines discrimination against women as:

> Discrimination against women" means any distinction, exclusion or restriction or any differential treatment based on sex and whose objectives or effects compromise or destroy the recognition, enjoyment or the exercise by women, regardless of their marital status, of human rights and fundamental freedoms in all spheres of life.[260]

The provision is quite similar to CEDAW's save for the obvious absence of the phrase "on a basis of equality of men and women". The African provision also sets out the measures, legislative, institutional and others, which State parties are to take to combat all forms of discrimination against women. These are to include the principle of equality in national constitutions and other legislation, enact and effectively implement appropriate legislative or regulatory measures, including those prohibiting or curbing all forms of discrimination against women and integrate gender perspectives in policy decisions, development plans, programs and activities in all spheres of life.[261] In addition, States are required to provide public education and information to eliminate harmful cultural and traditional practices.[262] Finally, the Protocol places an obligation on the State parties to take specific positive action to promote participative

257 *Id.* at Art. 13.

258 *Id.* at Art. 13(2), "subject to available resources".

259 *Id.* at Art. 4.

260 Art. 1(f), Protocol to the African Charter on Human and Peoples' Rights on the Rights of Women, 2003.

261 *Id.* at Art. 2.

262 *Id.* at Art. 2(2). *See also* Art. 5.

governance and the equal participation of women in political life, at all levels, in their countries through affirmative action.[263]

The Organisation of American States

The 1948 Charter of the Organisation of American States (OAS) established the Organisation that has the purposes, among others, to strengthen peace and security of the continent, to promote economic, social and cultural development and to seek the solution of political, juridical and economic problems that may rise among them. Among the Charter's principles is the clear proclamation of the fundamental rights of the individual without distinction as to race, nationality, creed or sex,[264] explicitly referring to non-discrimination. Like the OAU, the OAS Charter sets forth the purposes of defending sovereignty, territorial integrity, independence[265] and non-interference.[266] Although the OAS Charter does not mention human rights, except for when it refers to the Inter-American Commission on Human Rights and its functions, the OAS has adopted various treaties encompassing human rights. These include the American Convention on Human Rights, the Inter-American Declaration on the Rights and Duties of Man, the Inter-American Convention on the Elimination of all Forms of Discrimination against Persons with Disabilities. Finally, the OAS categorises itself as a regional agency within the United Nations.[267]

The American Convention on Human Rights

The Convention's intention is to consolidate, within the framework of democratic institutions, personal liberty and social justice based on respect for the essential rights of man where these essential rights are not derived from a person's nationality, but are based on attributes of the human personality.[268] The Convention also refers to the UDHR and "other international instruments."[269]

The Convention is divided into three parts: the general obligations, civil and political rights and economic, social and cultural rights. The clause on non-discrimination is first in line, whereas, similar to Article 2 ICCPR, the Convention obliges State parties to undertake to respect the rights and freedoms recognized therein and to ensure to all persons ("person" means every

263 *Id.* at Art. 9.
264 Art. 3, Charter of the Organisation of American States, 1948.
265 *Id.* at Art. 1.
266 *Id.* at Art. 2(b).
267 *Id.* at Art. 1.
268 Preamble, American Convention on Human Rights, 1969.
269 *Id.*

human being[270]) subject to their jurisdiction the free and full exercise of those rights and freedoms. Such is to occur, without any discrimination for reasons of race, colour, sex, language, religion, political or other opinion, national or social origin, economic status, birth, or any other social condition.[271] The provision refers to discrimination in enjoyment of the rights in the Convention. Therefore as stipulated in *Apitz Barbera et al. v Venezuela*,[272] discrimination with respect to the rights in the Convention constitutes a violation of Article 1(1) and the substantive right involved, implying that the article is "parasitic" as is Article 14 ECHR, and cannot stand independently. Furthermore, the Convention provides for equality before the law and entitlement, without discrimination, to equal protection of law.[273] The right to equality before the law requires equal application of the law, meaning judges and State officials must not act arbitrarily in enforcing laws, whereas the right to equal protection of law focuses on the content of law and directs legislators to avoid all discrimination when drafting and enacting statutes.[274] The latter can be likened to Article 26 ICCPR.[275]

As in the European and African human rights instruments, the list of grounds of discrimination set forth in Article 1 of the Convention is not exhaustive. This can de deduced from the phrase "any other social condition", leaving it as an open-ended list where other grounds can be added. The Inter-American Court on Human Rights (IACtHR) in *Atala Riffo and daughters v Chile*[276] concluded that there had been discrimination on the ground of sexual orientation, acknowledging that the list is not exhaustive but rather illustrative.

The Convention places an obligation on the State parties where the exercise of these rights is not already ensured by legislation or other provision, to adopt the provisions of the Convention with their constitutional processes, legislative measures as may be necessary.[277] The Convention does not provide for special measures or affirmative action, however, the IACtHR has stated that difference in treatment is not necessarily discriminatory. Such may be required to achieve justice or to protect persons requiring the application of special

---

270 *Id.* at Art. 1(2).

271 *Id.* at Art. 1(1).

272 Inter-American Court of Human Rights, No. 182, 5th August 2008, para. 209.

273 Art. 24, ACHR.

274 Thomas Antkowiak and Alejandra Gonza, The American Convention on Human Rights: Essential Rights (New York: Oxford University Press, 2017), 33.

275 For further details *see* Thomas Antkowiak and Alejandra Gonza, The American Convention on Human Rights: Essential Rights (New York: Oxford University Press, 2017), 33–34.

276 Series C, No. 239, Judgement of 24th February 2012, para. 85.

277 Art. 1(2), ACHR, 1969.

measures. That which is important is that such a distinction is based on reasonable and objective criteria and serves a legitimate state interest.[278]

The Convention also provides for rights in times of national emergencies such as war, public danger or other emergencies. Then the State parties may take measures derogating from their obligations under the convention, provide that the measures are not inconsistent with other obligations under international law and do not involve discrimination on the ground of race, colour, sex, language, religion, or social origin.[279] This is similar to the position of the ICCPR and reflects the significance of the non-discrimination principle. This is further demonstrated by the Inter-American Court of Human Rights that held that equality before the law, equal protection before the law and non-discrimination belong to *jus cogens*.[280]

The American Social Charter

The OAU adopted the American Social Charter (ASC) in 2012. The 2012 Charter is more focused on social development and social protections in the OAS member states, taking up economic, social and cultural rights and the essential role of human rights in the promotion of social development.[281] The aspirations of the Charter reflect the social nature of the rights incorporated, which include the elimination of hunger, illiteracy, broadening education, health care and public service as well as the elimination of discrimination. In addition is the explicit reference of the Charter to progressive measure in the full exercise of these rights. The ASC recognises the political atmosphere necessary for social development and thus refers to policies of good governance, transparency, citizen participation, accountability, just treatment before the law and fight against corruption.[282]

The ASC acknowledges the ethnic, racial, cultural, religious, linguistic diversity of the people of the Americas and thus incorporates the principle of non-discrimination by committing member states to promotion and protection of human rights and fundamental principles without distinction as to race, nationality, creed or sex.[283] The ASC places obligations on member states

278 *See* IACtHR, Advisory Opinion OC-4/84, "Proposed Amendment to the Naturalisation Provisions of the Constitution of Costa Rica" Series A No. 4, para. 56 (examining compliance of measures under the American Convention).

279 Art. 27, ACHR.

280 *Norín Catrimán et al. (Mapuche Indigenous People) v Chile*, Inter-American Court of Human Rights, No. 279, 29th May 2014, para. 197.

281 Preamble, American Social Charter, 2012.

282 *Id.*

283 *Id.*

to develop social protection policies and programs based on the principle of universality, solidarity equity and non-discrimination[284] and to eliminate gender, ethnic and racial discrimination.[285] The principle of non-discrimination cuts across the Charter in its various entitlements such as health,[286] adequate food[287] and education.[288]

Conclusion

The regional human rights treaties also provide important sources of non-discrimination protections. That which is unique about these treaties is that they are more or less adopted to the regional perspectives of human rights. This is to say, for example, that the African Charter is tailored more in line with the collective approach of African countries or governments to human rights. The same applies to the European and American Conventions. However, one similarity that cuts across all the regional instruments is the incorporation of the principles put forth in the UN Charter and the UDHR on the non-discrimination protections. In addition, the monitoring bodies of the regional instruments reference to the international human rights treaties and monitoring bodies in the interpretation of these rights. Another similarity is the expansion of the grounds of discrimination beyond the international grounds. Overall, the regional human rights system further the promotion of international human rights standards at the regional levels.

Part 4: Non-Discrimination Protections in National Frameworks

An African Perspective: South Africa

In as far as African perspectives are concerned; South Africa serves as an optimal example of the role of human rights in non-discrimination protections in national contexts. South Africa serves as a useful and unique case due to its diverse population[289] and long history of colonial conquest, racial

284 *Id.* at Art. 14.

285 *Id.* at Art. 15.

286 *Id.* at Art. 17.

287 *Id.* at Art. 18.

288 *Id.* at Art. 19.

289 It has a population of Black Africans (79%), White Africans (9.6%), Coloured Africans (8.9%) and Indians/Asians (2.5%).

discrimination, social injustice, political oppression, gender discrimination[290] and other social issues. It also serves as a demonstration of discrimination in a country that covers various discriminatory grounds as cited in human rights instruments.

The systematic discrimination in South Africa was through apartheid policy introduced in 1948, although racial discrimination dates from earlier on with the Dutch colonisation of the Cape of Good Hope in 1652.[291] Apartheid, meaning apartness in the Afrikaans language, was characterised by complete separation of the races, where segregated institutions, social and political, were established. In more practical terms, this meant segregated schools, hospitals, neighbourhoods, transport systems, etc. The central feature of this system was systematic discrimination/segregation of the majority black Africans by the minority white population. The policy of segregation generally separated races to the benefit of those of European descent and to the detriment of those of African descent.

What makes apartheid in South Africa unique is the systematic way in which the National Party, which came into power in 1948, formalised it through laws, which were often enforced with great brutality.[292] For example, The Bantu Education Act (1953) had the aim of enforcing racially separated education facilities. The Act's purpose was arguably to direct black or non-white youth to the unskilled labour market.[293] It established a Black Education Department in the Department of Native Affairs, which would compile a curriculum that suited the "nature and requirements of the black people."[294] The Group Areas Act (1950)[295] invoked physical separation between races by creating different residential areas for different races. This involved forceful removal of people living in areas other than those allocated to them. The Reservation of Separate Amenities Act (1953)[296] invoked segregation in all public amenities, public buildings, and public transport with the aim of eliminating contact between whites and other races. The Act stated that facilities provided for different races did not need to be equal. As for legislation related to labour law, the Bantu

290 Anne-Marie Mooney Cotter, Culture Clash: An International Legal Perspective on Ethnic Discrimination (New York: Routledge, 2016), 158.

291 Nancy L. Clark and William H. Worger, South Africa: The Rise and Fall of Apartheid 3rd Edition (New York: Routledge, 2016), 1.

292 *Id.*

293 *See* Ritha M Byrnes, South Africa: A Country Study (Washington D.C.: GPO for the Library of Congress, 1996).

294 Bantu Education Act, Act No. 47, 1953.

295 Act No. 41 of 1950.

296 Act No. 49 of 1953.

Building Workers Act (1951)[297] granted permission to blacks to be trained as artisans in the building industry, something previously reserved for whites. However, sections 15 and 19 precluded Whites from employing Africans in their homes to perform skilled jobs such as bricklaying and carpentry. Africans who performed skilled jobs outside those that had been allocated were guilty of an offence unless special permission had been granted. The Native Labour (Settlement of Disputes) Act[298] prohibited labour strikes by black people. Finally, the Natives (Abolition of Passes and Co-ordination of Documents) Act[299] (commonly known as the Pass Law) forced black people to carry identification passes with them at all times. These passes included a photograph, details of place of origin, employment record, tax payments, and encounters with the police. It was a criminal offence to be unable to produce a pass when required to do so by the police. No black person could leave a rural area for an urban one without a permit from the local authorities. On arrival in an urban area, a permit to seek work had to be obtained within 72 hours.[300]

In as far as international human rights are concerned, one cannot ignore the role of the international community in the elimination of apartheid in South Africa. Among the many measures the United Nations took to end apartheid,[301] two stand out. First is 1966 when the UNGA declared apartheid

297 Act No. 27 of 1951.

298 Act No. 48, 1953.

299 Act No. 67, 1952.

300 *Id.*

301 On the 2nd December 1950, the General Assembly declared that "a policy of 'racial segregation' (apartheid) is necessarily based on doctrines of racial discrimination" (Resolution 395(V)). On the 1st April 1960, the Security Council, in its first action on South Africa, adopted Resolution 134 deploring the policies and actions of the South African government in the wake of the killing of 69 peaceful African protesters in Sharpeville by the police on 21 March. The Council called upon the government to abandon its policies of apartheid and racial discrimination. On the 7th August 1963, the Security Council adopted Resolution 181 calling upon all States to cease the sale and shipment of arms, ammunition and military vehicles to South Africa. The arms embargo was made mandatory on the 4th November 1977. On the 13th November 1963, the General Assembly, in Resolution 1899(XVIII) on the question of Namibia, urged all States to refrain from supplying petroleum to South Africa. It was the first of many efforts by the UN to enact effective oil sanctions against apartheid On the 2nd December 1968, the General Assembly requested all States and organisations "to suspend cultural, educational, sporting and other exchanges with the racist regime and with organisations or institutions in South Africa which practice apartheid. On the 30th November 1973, the International Convention on the Suppression and Punishment of the Crime of Apartheid was approved by the General Assembly (Resolution 3068(XXVIII)). The convention came into force on the 18th July

as a "crime against humanity".[302] Second is the adoption of the Convention on the Suppression and Punishment of the Crime of Apartheid,[303] which has its roots in the opposition of the UN to the discriminatory racial policies of the South African government.[304] The Convention was the ultimate step in the condemnation of apartheid as it not only declared it unlawful because it violated the Charter of the UN, but in addition, it declared apartheid criminal.[305] All of these measures played a vital role in the elimination of apartheid. South Africa's first post-apartheid government, led by the African National Congress (ANC), embarked upon a nation-building project consciously predicated upon the creation of a "culture of human rights".[306] In an attempt to counter the legacy of grossly unequal allocation of resources, wealth and power, the South African government has made various legislative attempts to undo the effects of centuries of race-based oppression and marginalisation,[307] as discussed below.

The 1993 Interim Constitution

The 1993 interim constitution, as the name suggests, was a temporary constitution enacted prior to the adoption of the final Constitution of South

---

1976. On the 12th November 1974, the General Assembly suspended South Africa from participating in its work, due to international opposition to the policy of apartheid. South Africa was re-admitted to the UN in 1994 following its transition into a democracy. On the 17th August 1984, in Resolution 554, the Security Council declared null and void the new racist constitution of South Africa. On the 10th May 1994, South Africa's first democratically elected non-racial government took office following the general elections of 26–29 April. Available at UN website: un.org/en/events/mandeladay/apartheid.

302 *See* UNGA Resolution 2202 A (XXI), 16th December 1966. *See also* Resolution 556, 23rd October 1984.

303 30th November 1973. The Convention came into force on the 18th July 1976.

304 John Dugard, Convention on the Suppression and Punishment of the Crime of Apartheid at United Nations Audiovisual Library of International Law, United Nations, 2008, available at legal.un.org/avl/pdf/ha/cspca-e.pdf.

305 Art. 1 of the Convention "declares that apartheid is a crime against humanity and that inhuman acts resulting from the policies and practices of apartheid and similar policies and practices of racial segregation and discrimination are crimes violating the principles of international law". In addition, the art. "declares criminal those organisations, institutions and individuals committing the crime of apartheid".

306 Richard A. Wilson, "Reconciliation and Revenge in Post-Apartheid South Africa: Rethinking Legal Pluralism and Human Rights" 41:1 *Current Anthropology* (2000), 75–87, 76.

307 Anton Kok, "The Promotion of Equality and Prevention of Unfair Discrimination Act 4 of 2000: Proposals for Legislative Reform", 23:3 *South African Journal of Human Rights* (2008), 445–471, 445.

Africa. The Interim Constitution was drafted by the Multiparty Negotiating Forum[308] and enacted by the Parliament of South Africa. It provided for an end to white minority rule, a set of principles and a process for shaping a final constitution and a set of governing structures, which would oversee the transformation to a democracy.[309]

The Interim Constitution enumerated a bill of rights for the people of South Africa, as well as the establishment of the structures of national and provincial government, judiciary and other organisations to support democracy. The preamble of the Interim Constitution provides a view of the desired post-apartheid South Africa, where there was "a need to create a new order in which all South Africans will be entitled to a common South African citizenship in a sovereign and democratic constitutional state in which there is equality between men and women and people of all races so that all citizens shall be able to enjoy and exercise their fundamental rights and freedoms."[310] The rest of the preamble provides for logistics for the adoption of a final constitution. This clearly reflects the fact that the basic founding principles in this period were non-discrimination, human rights and democracy.

Coming to the provisions in the Constitution, the third chapter of the Constitution provides for fundamental rights:

(1) Every person shall have the right to equality before the law and to equal protection of the law.

(2) No person shall be unfairly discriminated against, directly or indirectly, and, without derogating from the generality of this provision, on one or more of the following grounds in particular: race, gender, sex, ethnic or social origin, colour, sexual orientation, age, disability, religion, conscience, belief, culture or language.

(3)(a) This section shall not preclude measures designed to achieve the adequate protection and advancement of persons or groups or categories of persons disadvantaged by unfair discrimination, in order to enable their full and equal enjoyment of all rights and freedoms.[311]

---

308 A forum comprising of political parties, national and homeland government representatives and traditional leaders that negotiated and laid down the principles and institutions as well as the interim constitution subsequent to the end of apartheid.

309 Alexander Johnston, "South Africa: The Election and the Transition Process—Five Contradictions in Search of a Resolution", 15:2 Third World Quarterly (1994), 187–204, 187.

310 Constitution of the Republic of South Africa, 1993.

311 Art. 8, Constitution of South Africa, 1993.

The schedules of the Constitution, which as a part complements it with additional details not mentioned in the provisions/articles, further elaborates the anti-discrimination rights. Schedule 4 has several outstanding articles in this regard. It provides for the establishment of one sovereign state, a common South African citizenship and a democratic system of government committed to achieving equality between men and women and people of all races[312] as well as a prohibition against racial, gender and all other forms of discrimination, and the promotion of racial and gender equality and national unity.[313] Again, equality before the law is guaranteed and includes laws, programmes or activities that have as their object, the amelioration of the conditions of the disadvantaged, including those disadvantaged on the grounds of race, colour or gender.[314]

Finally, in addition to articles on separation of powers between the legislature, executive and judiciary, the Schedule outlines the crucial role of the judiciary as having the power and jurisdiction to safeguard and enforce the Constitution and all fundamental rights in a qualified, independent and impartial setting.[315] The Interim Constitution was in force from the 27th April 1994 to the 4th February 1997.

The 1996 Constitution of the Republic of South Africa

The country's Constitutional Assembly adopted the Constitution of the Republic of South Africa in May 1996. As an integration of ideas from ordinary citizens, civil society and political parties represented in and outside of the Constitutional Assembly, it represents the collective wisdom of the people and has been arrived at by general agreement, thus giving it a character of legitimacy, credibility and accepted by South Africans.

To begin with, the preamble of the Constitution highlights the country's dark past but very bright future in terms of human rights and equality. It states that in recognition of "the injustices of our past ... adopt this Constitution as the supreme law of the Republic so as to heal the divisions of the past and establish a society based on democratic values, social justice and fundamental human rights: Lay the foundation for a democratic and open society in which ... every citizen is equally protected by law".[316]

312 Art. I, Schedule 4, Constitution of South Africa.

313 Art. III, Schedule 4, Constitution of South Africa, 1993.

314 *Id.* at Art. V.

315 *Id.* at Art. VII.

316 Preamble, The Constitution of the Republic of South Africa, 1996.

Of great essence is Chapter 2 containing the Bill of Rights. In as far as non-discrimination is concerned, Article 9 states:

1. Everyone is equal before the law and has the right to equal protection and benefit of the law.
2. Equality includes the full and equal enjoyment of all rights and freedoms. To promote the achievement of equality, legislative and other measures designed to protect or advance persons, or categories of persons, disadvantaged by unfair discrimination may be taken.
3. The state may not unfairly discriminate directly or indirectly against anyone on one or more grounds, including race, gender, sex, pregnancy, marital status, ethnic or social origin, colour, sexual orientation, age, disability, religion, conscience, belief, culture, language and birth.
4. No person may unfairly discriminate directly or indirectly against anyone on one or more grounds in terms of subsection (3). National legislation must be enacted to prevent or prohibit unfair discrimination.
5. Discrimination on one or more of the grounds listed in subsection (3) is unfair unless it is established that the discrimination is fair.[317]

As with the ACHPR, the grounds of discrimination include ethnic origin. Discrimination on the ground of disability is another interesting feature. The right to equality is listed as a non-derogable right in Article 37, which provides for states of emergency. However, this is not absolute as it only applies solely on the grounds of race, colour, ethnic or social origin, sex, religion or language.

Another feature of the Constitution is that the right to non-discrimination cuts across many of the other rights provided for in the Bill of Rights, emphasizing its central theme in the rights and freedoms in post-apartheid South Africa. For example, Article 16 provides for freedom of expression, but has an explicit exception to the effect that the right does not extend to advocacy of hatred that is based on race, ethnicity, gender or religion, and constitutes incitement to cause harm.[318] Similarly, Article 29 provides for the right to education and stresses the importance of taking into account the need to redress the results of past racially discriminatory laws and practices.[319] It also extends the right to establish independent educational institutions that, among other things, do not discriminate on the basis of race.[320] With regards to property

317 Art. 9, Constitution of the Republic of South Africa, 1996.

318 *Id.* at Art. 16(2)(c).

319 *Id.* at Art. 29(2)(c).

320 *Id.* at Art. 29(3)(a).

rights, the Constitution sets forth property redress for people whose tenure of land is legally insecure or people/communities dispossessed of property as a result of past racially discriminating laws or practices.[321]

Affirmative action is also one of the Constitutional concepts. Article 9(2) states,

> Equality includes the full and equal enjoyment of all rights and freedoms. To promote the achievement of equality, legislative and other measures designed to protect or advance persons, or categories of persons, disadvantaged by unfair discrimination may be taken.[322]

This section creates a broad category for beneficiaries of affirmative action, namely people who have been "disadvantaged" by unfair discrimination and no specific factors are used to connote disadvantage and no specific categories of disadvantaged people are mentioned.[323]

Finally, the Constitution in guaranteeing the rights enumerated, provides for the powers of courts, where the rights in the Bill of rights have been infringed.[324] An important aspect of the Constitution is the establishment of various state institutions supporting constitutional democracy in its Chapter 9. These include the Public Protector, The Human Rights Commission, Commission for the Protection of the Rights of Cultural, Religious and Linguistic Communities, Commission for Gender Equality etc. In context of this discussion on the human rights protections against discrimination, the Human Rights and Gender Equality Commissions draw attention. The Human Rights Commission has the task to promote respect for human rights and a culture of human rights; promote the protection, development and attainment of human rights; and monitor and assess the observance of human rights in the Republic.[325] The Commission also has the powers to investigate and to report on the observance of human rights, to take steps to secure appropriate redress where human rights have been violated, to carry out research, and to educate.[326]

---

321 *Id.* at Art. 25(6–7).

322 *Id.* at Art. 9(2).

323 Marié McGregor, "Affirmative Action and Non-Discrimination: South African Law Evaluated Against International Law" 39:3 *The Comparative and International Law Journal of Southern Africa* (2006), 397.

324 *Id.* at Art. 172.

325 *Id.* at Art. 184(1).

326 *Id.* at Art. 184(2).

The South African Constitution has three central values that transcend through all the rights and obligations encompassed in it; equality (or non-discrimination), human rights and democracy. This does not come as a surprise, considering the country's history and past challenges in the enjoyment of the right to non-discrimination. It is crucial to look into national legislation framework that comprehends these rights.

The Promotion of Equality and Prevention of Unfair Discrimination Act, 2000

The Promotion of Equality and Prevention of Unfair Discrimination Act was established to give substance to the constitutional commitments to equality, by providing a legal mechanism with which to confront, address and remedy past and present forms of incidental, institutional or structural unfair discrimination or inequality.[327] As discrimination and equality are probably two of the greatest social ills South African society has ever suffered, the Act seeks to underscore the primacy of equality and the historic struggle against discrimination as a foundational element of the liberatory ethic in South Africa.[328]

The Preamble of the Act sets out the context in which it is enacted where, citing the Constitution, it looks to eradication of social and economic inequalities, especially those systemic by nature, which were generated in the country's history by colonialism, apartheid and patriarchy. It further displays its character as a legislation to prevent or prohibit unfair discrimination and promote equality. It also invokes a very important aspect of the measures taken in post-apartheid South Africa: advancement, special legal and other measures of historically disadvantaged individuals, communities and social groups. The preamble sets forth the values of equality, fairness, equity, social progress, justice, human dignity and freedom.[329] The preamble also makes due note of the country's international obligations under binding treaties and customary international law in the field of human rights which promote equality and prohibit unfair discrimination, such as obligations specified in the Convention on the Elimination of All Forms of Discrimination Against Women and the Convention on the Elimination of All Forms of Racial Discrimination.[330]

---

327 Cathi Albertyn, Beth Goldblatt and Christopher Roederer, *Introduction to the Promotion of Equality and Prevention of Unfair Discrimination Act 4 of 2000* (Johannesburg: Witwatersrand University Press, 2001), 3.

328 Barney Pityana, "The Promotion of Equality and Prevention of Unfair Discrimination Act 4 of 2000", *Codicillus* No. 1, University of South Africa, 15th October 2002, 4.

329 Preamble, Promotion of Equality and Prevention of Unfair Discrimination Act.

330 *Id.*

The Act, given its purpose of "giving effect to the letter and spirit of the Constitution", and in particular section 9,[331] defines discrimination as any act or omission, including a policy, law, rule, practice, condition or situation which directly or indirectly imposes burdens, obligations or disadvantage on; or withhold benefits, opportunities or advantages from any person on one or more of the prohibited grounds.[332] The prohibited grounds are listed as being race, gender, sex, pregnancy, marital status, ethnic or social origin, colour, sexual orientation, age, disability, religion, conscience, belief, culture, language and birth; or any other ground where discrimination based on that other ground causes or perpetuates systemic disadvantage, undermines human dignity, or adversely affects the equal enjoyment of a person's rights and freedoms in a serious manner that is comparable to discrimination.[333] Chapter 2 of the Act comprehensively provides for the prohibited grounds of discrimination, following a prohibition on unfair discrimination by the State or any person against anyone.[334]

As for the ground of race, prohibition on this ground includes the dissemination of any propaganda or idea, which propounds the racial superiority or inferiority of any person. This includes incitement to, or participation in, any form of racial violence; the engagement in any activity which is intended to promote, or has the effect of promoting, exclusivity, based on race. The exclusion of persons of a particular race group under any rule or practice is prohibited where the rule or policy appears to be legitimate but actually aims at maintaining exclusive control by a particular race group. Also prohibited is the provision or continued provision of inferior services to any racial group, compared to those of another racial group; the denial of access to opportunities, including access to services or contractual opportunities for rendering services for consideration, or failing to take steps to reasonably accommodate the needs of such persons.[335]

The prohibition of discrimination on the ground of gender focuses more on the rights of women. It includes gender-based violence; female genital mutilation; the system of preventing women from inheriting family property; any practice, including traditional, customary or religious practice, which impairs the dignity of women and undermines equality between women and men, including the undermining of the dignity and well-being of the girl child. Also

331 This also includes sec.s 10 and 16(2)(c).

332 Sec. 1, Promotion of Equality and Prevention of Unfair Discrimination Act, 2000.

333 *Id.* at sec. 1(1)(xxii).

334 *Id.* at sec. 6.

335 *Id.* at sec. 7.

prohibited are policies or conduct that unfairly limit access of women to land rights, finance, and other resources; discrimination on the ground of pregnancy; limiting women's access to social services or benefits, such as health, education and social security; the denial of access to opportunities, including access to services or contractual opportunities for rendering services for consideration, or failing to take steps to reasonably accommodate the needs of such persons; systemic inequality of access to opportunities by women as a result of the sexual division of labour.[336]

The Act defines disability discrimination as denying or removing from any person who has a disability, any supporting or enabling facility necessary for their functioning in society. This also includes contravening the code of practice or regulations of the South African Bureau of Standards that govern environmental accessibility, as well as failing to eliminate obstacles that unfairly limit or restrict persons with disabilities from enjoying equal opportunities or failing to take steps to reasonably accommodate the needs of such persons.[337]

In addition to the prohibited grounds, the Act also prohibits hate speech,[338] harassment[339] as well as dissemination and publication of information that unfairly discriminates,[340] save for *bona fide* engagement in artistic creativity, academic and scientific inquiry, fair and accurate reporting in the public interest or publication of any information, advertisement or notice in accordance with section 16 of the Constitution.

The Act also covers the issue of unfair discrimination, which is when measures which are designed to protect or advance persons or categories of persons disadvantaged by unfair discrimination or the members of such groups or categories of persons are taken.[341] In determining such discrimination, the Act provides factors to be taken into account,[342] where hate speech and harrasment

---

336 *Id.* at sec. 8.

337 *Id.* at sec. 9.

338 *Id.* at sec. 10.

339 *Id.* at sec. 11. Harassment means unwanted conduct which is persistent or serious and demeans, humiliates or creates a hostile or intimidating environment or is calculated to induce submission by actual or threatened adverse consequences and which is related to sex, gender or sexual orientation; or a person's membership or presumed membership of a group identified by one or more of the prohibited grounds or a characteristic associated with such group, *see* sec. 1(1)(xiii).

340 *Id.* at sec. 12.

341 *Id.* at Art. 14(1).

342 Whether the discrimination impairs or is likely to impair human dignity; the impact or likely impact of the discrimination on the complainant; the position of the complainant in society and whether he or she suffers from patterns of disadvantage or belongs

are explicitly excluded from the ambit of this protection.[343] Interesting is the establishment of Equality Courts, which are not separate or specialised courts, but rather magistrates and the High Court in which the Act endows these powers in their respective areas of jurisdiction.[344] The courts have the function of determining, in proceedings instituted under the Act, whether unfair discrimination, hate speech or harassment has taken place as alleged.[345]

Finally, the Act places a duty on the State to promote equality, with the help of the relevant constitutional institutions. This involves development of awareness of fundamental rights in order to promote a climate of understanding, mutual respect and equality. The State is also to take measures to develop and implement programmes in order to promote equality; and where necessary or appropriate, to develop action plans to address any unfair discrimination, hate speech or harassment. It is to enact further legislation that seeks to promote equality and to establish a legislative framework in line with the objectives of the Act, develop codes of practice as contemplated in the Act in order to promote equality, and develop guidelines, including codes in respect of reasonable accommodation, provide assistance, advice and training on issues of equality, and develop appropriate internal mechanisms to deal with complaints of unfair discrimination, hate speech or harassment and conduct information campaigns to popularise the Act.[346]

Non-Discrimination in Employment: The 1998 Employment Equity Act

The 1998 Employment Equity Act has the aim of achieving equity in the workplace by promoting equal opportunity and fair treatment in employment through the elimination of unfair discrimination; and implementing affirmative action measures to redress the disadvantages in employment experienced

to a group that suffers from such patterns of disadvantage; the nature and extent of the discrimination; whether the discrimination is systemic in nature; whether the discrimination has a legitimate purpose; whether and to what extent the discrimination achieves its purpose; whether there are less restrictive and less disadvantageous means to achieve the purpose; whether and to what extent the respondent has taken such steps as being reasonable in the circumstances to address the disadvantage which arises from or is related to one or more of the prohibited grounds; or accommodate diversity, *see id.* at sec. 14(3).

343 *Id.* at sec. 15.

344 *Id.* at sec. 16.

345 *Id.* at sec. 21.

346 *Id.* at sec. 25.

by designated groups, in order to ensure their equitable representation in all occupational categories and levels in the workforce.[347]

As a reflection of the discriminatory nature of labour relations that had existed during apartheid, the Act's preamble acknowledges the disparities in employment, occupation and income in the country's labour market, rendering the mere repeal of discriminatory laws insufficient redress.[348] Again, in the light of the constitutional right to equality extensively discussed above, the Act sets out to eliminate unfair discrimination in employment and ensure the implementation of employment equity to redress the effects of discrimination.[349] Striking in regards to the values embodied by the Act is that of "giving effect to the obligations of the Republic as a member of the International Labour Organisation."[350] To this effect, the Act is to be interpreted, not only in compliance with the Constitution, but also in compliance with the international law obligations of the Republic, in particular those contained in the International Labour Organisation Convention (No. 111, 1958) concerning Discrimination in Respect of Employment and Occupation.[351] The incorporation of the obligations arising from international labour law (ILO conventions) makes the human rights drive behind this legislation apparent.

In as far as discrimination in employment is concerned, there are three aspects that are central in the Act; elimination, prohibition and affirmative action. These aspects are embodied in sections 5, 6(1) and 6(2) respectively. The elimination clause places a duty on the employer to take steps to promote equal opportunity in the workplace by eliminating unfair discrimination in any employment policy or practice.[352] As for the aspect of prohibition, the Act states:

> 6.(1) No person may unfairly discriminate, directly or indirectly, against an employee, in any employment policy or practice, on one or more grounds, including race, gender, sex. pregnancy, marital status, family responsibility, ethnic or social origin, colour, sexual orientation, age, disability, religion, HIV status, conscience, belief, political opinion, culture, language and birth.

---

347 Sec. 2, Employment Equity Act, 1998.

348 Preamble, Employment Equity Act, 1998.

349 *Id.*

350 *Id.*

351 Sec. 3, Employment Equity Act, 1998.

352 *Id.* at sec. 5.

In *Leonard Dingler Employee Representative Council and others v Leonard Dingler (PTY) Ltd*,[353] all the white employees were paid on a monthly basis, irrespective of their job title, rank or length of service. In contrast, black employees (the applicants) were paid on a weekly basis, and were only "promoted" to monthly pay depending on their length of service, job title and rank and even so, only a handful of black employees had been promoted to monthly pay. In addition, there were different benefit funds in place for the categories of employees. The membership of the Staff Benefit Fund comprised of predominantly white employees, paid on a monthly basis and the employer made a 10% contribution to this Fund. On the other hand, the Pension Fund comprised only of black employees, paid on a weekly basis and the employer made on 5% contributions to this Fund. The employees sent a letter to the employer, requesting that they be allowed to join the Staff Benefit Fund, which they were denied on the ground that it was limited to employees paid on a monthly basis, though the rules did not stipulate such an admission criteria. The Labour Court held that the employer's interpretation and its application of the rules of the Staff Benefit Fund amounted to unfair discrimination based of race, contrary to section 6 of the Employment Equity Act, which at the time of the judgement had repealed item 2(1) (a) of Schedule 7 of the Labour Relations Act.

Affirmative action is an aspect also articulated in the Constitution.[354] Article 6(2) provides that it is not unfair discrimination to take affirmative action measures consistent with the purposes of the Act or to distinguish, exclude or prefer any person on the basis of an inherent requirement of a job. However, this must be read alongside section 15, which provides for the definition, scope and limitation of affirmative action. It defines affirmative action as measures designed to ensure that suitably qualified people from designated groups have equal employment opportunities and are equitably represented in all occupational categories and levels in the workforce of a designated employer. This includes measures to identify and eliminate employment barriers, including unfair discrimination, which adversely affect people from designated groups; measures designed to further diversity in the workplace based on equal dignity and respect of all people; measures making reasonable accommodation for people from designated groups in order to ensure that they enjoy equal opportunities and are equitably represented in the workforce of a designated employer; measures to ensure the equitable representation of suitably qualified people from designated groups in all occupational categories and levels in the workforce; and measures to retain and develop people from designated

353 (1997) 11 BLLR 1438 (LC).

354 *See* Art. 9(2), Constitution of the Republic of South Africa, 1996.

groups and to implement appropriate training measures, including measures in terms of an Act of Parliament providing for skills development. It is crucial to note that the last two measures include preferential treatment and numerical goals, but not quotas.

In clarifying 'suitably qualified people from designated groups', the Labour Court stated in *Public Servants Association obo Tlowana v MEC of Agriculture*, where a candidate to a position was shortlisted and granted the position (where the preference was a woman) despite the fact that she did not meet the very minimum requirements and the applicant to the case successfully challenged the appointment,[355] that:

> Opening the post to all groups does not mean that a higher standard applies when assessing suitability and merits for posts for non-designated groups than when posts are restricted to designated groups. Applying a higher standard for non-designated groups implies that a lower standard is use to appoint persons from designated groups. By implication less suitable and less meritorious people fill posts reserved for designated groups. That cannot be the intention or the letter and spirit of the Employment Equity Act. Equality means fairness and justice, to the candidate and to the people they serve. Fairness and justice cannot prevail if candidates who are less than best, who are less suitable and less meritorious are appointed.[356]

The Act also provides for the burden of proof in cases of discrimination. It requires that whenever unfair discrimination is alleged in terms of the Act, the employer against whom the allegation is made must establish that it is fair.[357] In *Daniel Ntai & two others v South African Breweries Ltd*, it was stated that the application of an affirmative action policy constitutes merely a shield or defence. An employer may rely upon such defence should the employer be challenged on the basis of a reverse discrimination when the employer implements an affirmative action policy to advance and protect employees or groups or categories of employees who were disadvantaged by unfair discrimination in the past, in order to enable their full and equal enjoyment of all rights and freedoms. However, there is no legal obligation or duty on an employer to implement affirmative action and therefore, by the same token, such employees

355 Case No. JR 868/10.

356 *South African Police Services v Zandberg* (2010) 2 BLLR 194 (LC), para. 198.

357 Sec. 11, Employment Equity Act, 1998.

simply acquire no right to affirmative action.[358] The EEA puts in place various mechanisms to ensure that the rights encompassed are implemented. These include establishment of a Commission for Employment Equity,[359] employment equity plans[360] and labour inspection.[361]

The Employment Equity Act has addressed many issues in as far as discrimination in employment is concerned. It reflects the principles of the Constitution and the efforts of the post-apartheid era in eliminating discrimination in the

358 Case No. J 4476/99, para. 86.

359 Sec.s 28 and 30, Employment Equality Act, 1998.The Commission has the functions to advise the Minister on codes of good practice, regulations made by the Minister and policy and any other matter concerning the Act. In addition, the Commission may make awards recognising achievements of employers in furthering the purpose of the Act, research and report to the Minister on any matter relating to the application of the Act including appropriate and well-researched norms and benchmarks for the setting of numerical goals in various sectors, and perform any other prescribed function.

360 Employers must prepare and implement an employment equity plan which will achieve reasonable progress towards employment equity in that employer's workforce. The employment equity plan must state the objectives to be achieved for each year of the plan; the affirmative action measures to be implemented as required by sec. 15(2); where underrepresentation of people from designated groups has been identified by the analysis, the numerical goals to achieve the equitable representation of suitably qualified people from designated groups within each occupational category and level in the workforce, the timetable within which this is to be achieved, and the strategies intended to achieve those goals; the timetable for each year of the plan for the achievement of goals and objectives other than numerical goals; the duration of the plan, which may not be shorter than one year or longer than five years; the procedures that will he used to monitor and evaluate the implementation of the plan and whether reasonable progress is being made towards implementing employment equity; the internal procedures to resolve any dispute about the interpretation or implementation of the plan; the persons in the workforce, including senior managers, responsible for monitoring and implementing the plan; and any other prescribed matter, *id.* at sec. 20(1–2).

361 A labour inspector acting in terms of this Act has the authority to enter, question and inspect as provided for in sec.s 65 and 66 of the Basic Conditions of Employment Act. A labour inspector must request and obtain a written undertaking from a designated employer to comply with paragraphs *(a) to (j) of sec. 36* within a specified period, if the inspector has reasonable grounds to believe that the employer has failed to consult with employees as required by sec. 16, conduct an analysis as required by sec. 19, prepare an employment equity plan as required by sec. 20, implement its employment equity plan, submit an annual report as required by sec. 21, publish its report as required by sec. 22, prepare a successive employment equity plan as required by sec. 23, assign responsibility to one or more senior managers as required by sec. 24, inform its employees as required by sec. 25 or keep records as required by sec. 26. *See* sec.s 35 and 36.

country, as provided for by not only the national legislation, but by the ILO conventions.

Conclusion

The case of South Africa is one of great interest in as far as treatment of equality and non-discrimination on the national level in part as a result of the international human rights law. Because of the country's history, many different forms of discrimination have been identified in the national legal system. Again, it is of interest because the anti-discrimination national legislation, including the Constitution, draw heavily from the rights, obligations and measures encompassed in the international human rights standards discussed herein, both general and specialized, and provide a glimpse of how these can be applied in the national context.

An American Perspective: Brazil

As far as non-discrimination rights are concerned, Brazil also offers an interesting case study, due to the historical aspects associated with the country's approach to non-discrimination today. One of these aspects is the North Atlantic slave trade that dominated the Americas for three hundred years. Brazil was one of the largest importers of Africans slaves and the last country in the western hemisphere to abolish slave trade in 1888.[362]

Another aspect from a discrimination perspective is the colonization of Brazil by the Portuguese and their subsequent settlement in Brazil. As opposed to family-based colonization in North America, most of the Portuguese settlers were male and often sought out African mixed or indigenous females as mates.[363] This history of miscegenation has resulted in Brazil's diverse racial elements in the population. As opposed to South African apartheid case where there were strict racially—specific laws and policies based on segregation and thus, almost non-existent inter-marriages, miscegenation in Brazil suggests "fluid race relations".[364] This diverse racial component of the Brazilian population has raised challenges in regards to discrimination in the country. This section explores how the various non-discrimination rights previously discussed have been implemented in Brazil. It is equally important to state that Brazil had previously been considered as a "racial democracy" where the pernicious

---

362 Edward Telles, "Racial Discrimination and Miscegenation: The Experience in Brazil" 44:3 UN Chronicle (2007), 1.

363 *Id.*

364 *Id.*

effects of race had no place.[365] However, the society in recent year has recognized various forms of inequality and taken some measures to address it.

The Constitution of Federative Republic of Brazil

The preamble of The Constitution of Federative Republic of Brazil (*Constituição da República Federativa do Brasil*) defines the supreme values or principles as being liberty, security, well-being, development, equality and justice in a democratic state and a traditional, pluralist and unprejudiced society.[366] In addition, the Constitution provides for the objectives of the country as among others to promote the well-being of all without prejudice as to origin, race, sex, colour, age and any other form of discrimination.[367] It is interesting that the constitution incorporates the principle of non-discrimination, although it makes no reference to international standards of human rights on this principle, despite one of the principles the Constitution being the prevalence of human rights.[368] However, the Constitution provides that the rights and guarantees established in the constitution do not exclude others derived from the regime and principles adopted by it, or from international treaties to which Brazil is party.[369]

Article 5 of the Constitution also provides for equality before the law, with no distinction whatsoever to all (Brazilians and foreigners residing in the country). The right of equality is also categorized as an inviolable right under the Constitution,[370] where men and women have equal rights.[371] More relevant to labour or employment are the notions that that principles upon which the country is founded include the social values of work and free initiative.[372]

Coming to the issue of equality to employment, these rights are found in chapter II of the Constitution dealing with social rights. This chapter is very comprehensive and covers many human rights at work such as the rights to leisure, right to safe working environment, right to join workers' or employers' organisations and the right to strike.[373] The right to equal pay for work is provided for by requiring a salary floor in proportion to the extent and complexity

365 Stanley R. Bailey, "Brazil", The Wiley Blackwell Encyclopedia of Race, Ethnicity and Nationalism (2015) DOI: 10.1002/9781118663202, 106.

366 Preamble, Constitution of Brazil 1988.

367 *Id.* at Art. 3(IV).

368 *Id.* at Art. 4(II).

369 *Id.* at Art. 5(LXXVII)(2*).

370 *Id.* at Art. 5.

371 *Id.* at Art. 5(I).

372 *Id.* at Art. 1(IV).

373 *Id.* at Art.s 7 to 11.

of the work,[374] and the prohibition of any difference in pay in the performance of the duties and in hiring criteria by reasons of sex, age, colour or marital status,[375] as well as prohibition to any discrimination with respect to pay and hiring criteria for handicapped workers.[376]

The Constitution demonstrates the dualist approach by requiring that international treaties and conventions on human rights approved by both house of the national congress, in two different voting sessions by three-fifth votes of their respective members, shall be equivalent to constitutional Amendments.[377] The constitution also provides for punishment for the crime of discrimination where it states that all acts of discrimination against fundamental rights and liberties are to be punished by law[378] as well as that racism is a crime for which bail is not available and which is punishable by imprisonment pursuant to law.[379]

The Act against Racism

The Act Against Racism (*Lei Cao*), Law No. 7,716/89 is more of a penal law which provides for or deals with crimes resulting from race and colour discrimination and sets forth their specific punishments.[380] In other words, it deals with crimes resulting from prejudice as to race, colour, ethnic group, religion or national origin.[381] The Act also sanctions the preventing or hindering of access of a qualified person to any position in the public administration whether direct or indirect, as well as any public service concessionaries for reasons of discrimination or prejudice which are to be punishable by the penalty of imprisonment from two to five years.[382] Private companies are also punishable by imprisonment (2–5 years) where they deny or hinder employment for reasons of discrimination or prejudice.[383]

In *Public Prosecutor's Office v. Mei Fewg Xia*,[384] the complainant (Ms. Gusmao) was informed by her cousin that there was a vacancy at the defendant's commercial establishment and that the defendant had agreed to hire her subject

374 *Id.* at Art. 7(V).
375 *Id.* at Art. 7(XXX).
376 *Id.* at Art. 7(XXXI).
377 *Id.* at Art. 5(LXXVII)(3*).
378 *Id.* at Art. 5(XLI).
379 *Id.* at Art. 5(XLII).
380 Art. 1, Law No. 7.716/89.
381 *Id.*
382 *Id.* at Art. 3.
383 *Id.* at Art. 4.
384 Case No. 993.05.011926-2/00856085.3/5-0000-000, Judgment of 14th February 2008.

only to a personal interview to negotiate a salary. Upon arrival of the complainant at the establishment, the defendant started to scream racial slurs at the complainant, saying she would not hire her. The prosecutor argued a violation of Article 4 of the Law No. 7, 716/89 by the defendant. The court Appeal (being the court of second instance) reaffirmed the judgment of court of the first instance, which had sentenced the defendant to two years imprisonment. It concluded that the defendant denied employment to complainant due to her race.

Finally, Article 20 provides that practicing, inducing or inciting discrimination or prejudice on the basis on the race, colour, ethnic group, religion or national origin is to be punishable to imprisonment and a fine.[385] In addition, where these crimes are committed through the use of mass media or publications of any nature, the penalty is aggravated to imprisonment and impositions of a fine.[386]

Non-Discrimination in Employment: The Consolidation of Labour Laws

Labour Relations in Brazil are a matter of federal law, thus labour rights are nationally standardized, and apply regardless of an employer's place of business or place of incorporation.[387] The 1943 Consolidation of Labour Laws (Labour code) encompasses all labour laws regulating labour relationships in Brazil. It has been complemented, altered and amended over the years by statutes and by the 1988 Constitution. Interpretation of the Code by the Labour courts has influenced its application.

As far as the rights to non-discrimination are concerned, the law deals with the protection of women in work. The Act prohibits job advertisements containing any reference to sex, age, colour or family status save for when the nature of the work clearly requires such a reference. The Act also prohibits denial of employment or promotion or dismissal from employment by reason for sex, age, colour or family status, taking into account sex, sex, age, colour or family status as a determining factor in establishing compensation and professional development. Again, the Act prohibits the confirmation of sterilely or pregnancy by medical statement or test of any nature in connection with the

385 *Id.* at Art. 20(1).

386 *Id.* at Art. 20(2)(iii).

387 L&E Global, Employment Law Overview 2017: Brazil (Sao Paulo: Tozzini Freire Advogados, 2017).

employment or continuity in a job as well as intimate inspections on female employees by an employer or its representative.[388]

As for special measures or affirmative action, the Act states that its articles do not restrict the adoption of temporary measures aimed at establishing equality policies between men and women, especially those aimed at correcting distortions affecting professional formation, access to employment and general work conditions of women.[389]

Law No. 9.029/1995

This Act addresses discrimination at work, dealing with discrimination with regards to access to employment. The Act prohibits the adoption of any discrimination or limiting practice concerning access to employment, or its continuity, due to sex, origin, race, colour, marital states, family status or age.[390] The Act also provides of penalties associated with violations of the Law, which include administrative fines (amounting to ten times the higher salary paid by the employer) as well as prohibition from getting loans or financing with government/public financial institutions.[391]

Finally the Act provides that where an employment relationship has been disrupted due to a discriminatory act under the Law, the employee will have the option to either being readmitted to work plus receiving an amount equivalent to his/her salary for the receipt of twice the salary for that sum duration.[392] In *Paulo Roberto dos Reis Pereira v. Parmalat do Brasil s. A—Industria de Alimentor*,[393] the plaintiff filed a complaint against his former employer, alleging that he had been racially discriminated against by one of the defendant's representative s who had, during the term of the plaintiff's employment, called him derogatory names and words alluding to race and thus causing him humiliation and offending his honour and dignity. The defendant in his response claimed that it was usual for them to call each other by "nicknames" and the plaintiff had never shown displeasure. The superior Labour court ruled that the Brazilian laws (Article 3(IV) and Article 5 of the Constitution and law No. 9,029/95) as well as international rules, specifically Convention No. 111 of the ILO and the Declaration on Fundamental Principles and Rights at Work and its follow up, prohibit the adoption of any practice of prejudice or

388 Art. 373(A), Consolidation of Labour Laws, 1943.

389 *Id.*

390 Art. 1, Law No. 1 9.029/1995.

391 *Id.* at Art. 3.

392 *Id.* at Art. 4.

393 Case No. 01011-2001-561-04-00-5, Judgment of 10th August 2005.

discrimination. Again, the employer was held responsible for discriminatory acts of the representative during the performance of his professional activities because he was responsible for ensuring proper conduct in the work place. That which is interesting about this case is that despite the fact that the ILO conventions are not referred to in Brazil's constitution or non-discrimination legislation, the supreme Labour court still draws from these instruments when reaching a judgment.

Conclusion

The two national legal frameworks provide interesting insights as to how the international human rights standards are addressed at the national level. The national frameworks examined in this chapter present different approaches in dealing with discrimination on various grounds, considering not only the international obligations of the country, but also a number of social and historical factors. An interesting observation is the way by which the national legislation draws non-discrimination standards and interpretations directly from the international treaties and focuses on the international principles provided by these treaties, rather than paying much attention to the regional treaties. The South African case displays the application of international standards drawn from the Bill of Rights and the ILO Conventions in general aspects of non-discrimination as well as the specific case of employment. Neither is there mention of the regional standards, that is the African human rights treaties, nor the interpretations of the monitoring bodies. The same is true for Brazil, which is a member of the OAS. Despite the regional treaties being "closer" to the national contexts, the national legislation still appears to draw heavily from the international human rights treaties.

Final Remarks

This paper has looked at the principle of non-discrimination from an international human rights perspective by locating the right in various international and regional human rights instruments and the way it has been interpreted by the various monitoring bodies. Although the principle is one of the core principles in international law, it is also dynamic in the sense that it changes form with time to meet the specific needs of a period of time. This is demonstrated by the increasing number of protected grounds of discrimination as well as the rights on which discrimination can be invoked. As a final note, it is important to state that it is widely acknowledged that the right to non-discrimination has become a part of customary international law, and as such, binds all states, irrespective of their ratification of human rights treaties.[394]

Reading List

Albertyn, Cathi, Goldblatt, Beth, and Roederer, Christopher. *Introduction to the Promotion of Equality and Prevention of Unfair Discrimination Act 4 of 2000*. Johannesburg: Witwatersrand University Press, 2001.

Antkowiak, Thomas, and Gonza, Alejandra. *The American Convention on Human Rights: Essential Rights*. New York: Oxford University Press, 2017.

Clark, Nancy, and Worger, William. South Africa: *The Rise and Fall of Apartheid*. New York: Routledge.

Cotter, Anne-Marie Mooney. *Culture Clash: An International Legal Perspective on Ethnic Discrimination*. New York: Routledge, 2016.

Davidov, Guy, and Langille, Brian. eds. *The Idea of Labour. Law*. Oxford: Oxford University Press, 2011.

Dorssemont, Filip, Lörcher, Klaus, and Schömann, Isabellel. eds. *The European Convention on Human Rights and the Employment Relation*. Oxford: Hart Publishing, 2013.

Macklem, Patrick. *The Sovereignty of Human Rights*. New York: Oxford University Press, 2015.

Murray, Rachel. *Human Rights in Africa: From the OAU to the African Union*. New York: Cambridge University Press, 2004.

Nowak, Manfred. *U.N. Covenant on Civil and Political Rights: CCPR Commentary*. Virginia: Engel Publishers, 2005.

Valticos, Nicolas. *International Labour*. The Netherlands: Springer, 2013.

394 *See* Malcom Shaw, *International Law* (Cambridge: Cambridge University Press, 2008), 287; Daniel Moeckli, "Equality and Non-Discrimination" in Stephanie Farrior (ed.), *Equality and Non-Discrimination under International Law Vol. 2* (New York: Routledge, 2016), 57.

www.ingramcontent.com/pod-product-compliance
Lightning Source LLC
Chambersburg PA
CBHW031332230926
51848CB00001B/205
9789004345461